Instructor's Resource Manual

Instructor's Resource Manual

Kelly S. Mayhew
San Diego City College

to accompany

RACE, CLASS, AND GENDER IN THE UNITED STATES
AN INTEGRATED STUDY

Seventh Edition

Paula S. Rothenberg

WORTH PUBLISHERS

Instructor's Resource Manual
by Kelly S. Mayhew
to accompany
Rothenberg: Race, Class, and Gender in the United States, Seventh Edition

© 2007, 2004, 2001 by Worth Publishers

ISBN 13: 978-1-4292-0170-4
ISBN 10: 1-4292-0170-3

First Printing

Printed in the United States of America

Worth Publishers
41 Madison Avenue
New York, NY 10010
www.worthpublishers.com

Contents

Instructor's Resource Manual

General Introduction

The central argument that students will encounter in Paula Rothenberg's *Race, Class, and Gender in the United States*, seventh edition, is that categories of race, class, gender, and sexuality are socially constructed: they are neither natural, universal, nor inevitable, yet they have real effects on our lives. This means that everyone is subject to social processes. Hence, it is not just women who are gendered but also men. The experiences of heterosexuals, as well as gays and lesbians, are marked by their sexuality. White people, along with people of color, live racially structured lives. And class touches the middle class, as well as poor and working-class people. In other words, any system of differentiation shapes those on whom it bestows privilege as well as those it oppresses. Thus, in a social context in which white people have often viewed themselves as nonracial or racially neutral, it is crucial to look at the "racialness" of white experience. Likewise, in a context in which heterosexuality is viewed as normative (the unacknowledged default position), it is crucial to look at the construction of heterosexuality.

As I have shown in previous editions of this *Instructor's Resource Manual*, the process of thinking through social constructions is a complicated one and is best approached with certain strategies in mind. First, students will be asked to adopt a conscious process in which they think about race, class, and gender categories that they may have taken for granted as "real" or "true" in the sense that they seem permanent, immutable, or at least inevitable and thus not worth resisting. Second, students should consider their role in maintaining these inequities, whether they are on the side of privilege or not, and to attend carefully to the impact of these categories on themselves, on others, and on society at large. For some students, this process of reflection is already ongoing in their lives; for others, it will be a process initiated by you, their instructor. Such an initiation can be exciting and dynamic. It can also be painful or even threatening for students, so it is important to be aware of how fundamentally the materials and frameworks in this text can affect the ways students map out their world. Thus, some students will be moved to question themselves and the social categories of exclusion in which they live, and their questions might lead to political action. Others, however, after thinking through race, class, gender, and sexuality will continue justifying the status quo and rationalizing their place within it. All kinds of students will, nevertheless, benefit from the exposure to this material, as all of us, teachers as well as

1

students, need to be conscious of the histories and specificities of our cultural positions. The point of teaching material such as this is that it is, itself, part of the solution for social change.

Audience

As I discovered from the reception of previous editions of this manual, our challenge to appeal to a wide-ranging audience was successful. *Race, Class, and Gender in the United States*, seventh edition, tries to account for a student population that extends from elite universities to community colleges, from advanced to basic composition courses, from introductory women's studies courses to upper-division ethnic studies classes, from general education sociology or American Pluralism sections to courses designed for social work majors. I have tried to use the material that worked in the last edition, while adding fresh questions and assignments that not only account for the new essays in the seventh edition but also flesh out some areas that were in the previous manual. The fact that Rothenberg's text is taught in so many kinds of classrooms, to so many kinds of audiences, is testimony to its scope, its significance, and its necessity. I mention this, first, by way of reminding you of the good company you keep and, second, by way of explaining the structure of the assignments that follow.

Challenges for Students and Instructors

The primary emphasis in these assignments is to stimulate *critical thinking, analysis*, and *reflection*. Critical thinking, however, does not occur in a vacuum: the content on which thought processes act affects what knowledge is produced. Thus, I have repeatedly emphasized the specific kinds of thinking that the content of the book encourages: students will, hopefully, begin to *denaturalize*, through critical and historical investigation, categories that have come to constitute the seemingly natural; *understand*, through analysis, the process by which such mystification occurs; and *reflect* on the effects of racism, sexism, heterosexism, class discrimination, and the like. Therefore, the material and the assignments are challenging (i.e., difficult and sometimes intimidating). Students will have to work through and struggle with some hard concepts to make sense of what is at stake. The text will ask some students to radically revise their understanding of the world and its organization; hence, you should anticipate some resistance from them. Other students will feel that they have nothing to say, as they will recognize their relative privilege and (erroneously) conclude that because they have never "suffered" in the ways the people they read about have, they have nothing concrete to offer here. You can ask these students to focus on looking at the ways they may be privileged and recognize the epistemological implications: What knowledge have they lost or do they lose *because of* their privileges? For still others, the material will confirm things they have long suspected. Students who find their experiences reflected on the pages of

Race, Class, and Gender in the United States, seventh edition, can gain a vocabulary to describe the structure of their lives. In part because of the wide-ranging responses the material will elicit from different student populations, the writing exercises are designed to steer attention away from the students' own reactions to the materials and focus it instead on the structural issues at stake.

The Integrated Approach

The assignments are written in as broad a manner as possible, to be adapted to the needs of your classroom and curriculum. New to the seventh edition of the *Instructor's Resource Manual* are short, self-evaluation questions that can be used in conjunction with "clicker" technology or simply by asking students to respond anonymously on a piece of paper during class. Rothenberg's integrated approach to the theoretical concepts has been maintained at the pedagogical level as well; many of the assignments have been designed to connect with readings in other sections of the book. This approach has several advantages. First, it reminds students of concepts they have encountered elsewhere in the collection; or, if they haven't yet been exposed to that material, it may prompt them to look at it now. Second, for instructors assigning selective sections and sections in nonchronological order, this approach points out connections to useful pieces students may otherwise miss. The third, and perhaps the most important advantage of this integrated approach, is that it encourages students to explore the book on their own, to find pieces that speak to them. In my experience, this is one of the most useful aspects of teaching the book. In this process of discovery, even the most resistant students come to "own" certain writings that they'll recall long after the semester has passed. I highly recommend allowing, or even assigning, students to wander through the book at some point in the term.

Types of Assignments

The format of the assignments in this manual conforms roughly to the idea generation-writing-research model of college classroom writing. I kept to this general format so instructors in a wide variety of fields and disciplines will be able to adapt assignments to their needs quite readily. This three-part writing structure is highly flexible and has the advantage of not necessarily leading to a piece of writing as the finished product. For example, the "Generating Ideas/Small-Group Discussions" exercises can also be the basis of preparation for exams, and instructors can vary the assignments as needed for their specific disciplines. In addition, the assignment portion of this text has been directed at the student, so you may reproduce assignments directly from the manual and distribute them if you choose. Finally, as I mentioned earlier, I've added a few short self-assessment questions to the beginning of each section. These can be used in a "clicker" situation or for students to jot down responses before class discussion begins. They've been designed as a sort of interactive "temperature-taking" to get the students involved, especially if they are using this book in a large, lecture-style classroom setting.

The parts in the manual correspond with the parts of Rothenberg's book. Within each part, there are *Issues and Questions to Consider* that the instructor can use as the basis for freewriting exercises or classroom discussion; a *Generating Ideas/Small-Group Discussion* section that helps students begin the critical thinking, reading, and writing processes; *Writing Assignments* that focus on writing single essays; *Research/Analysis Projects*, some of which make connections to materials elsewhere in the collection and some that require outside research; and, finally, a *Recommended Media* section that provides some suggestions for films, documentaries, music, Internet sites, TV shows, and so on that can accompany and expand your use of the book. The idea-generating exercises can be used as the basis for classroom discussion or journal writing exercises. Several questions in each section ask students to draw connections between pieces. As I mentioned earlier, instructors who don't assign the entire book can still have students utilize materials from other areas. This approach also encourages students to draw on their own interests to explore the book.

Encouraging Critical Thinking

The primary focus in this manual has been on encouraging critical thinking, so in the assignments less attention has been placed on the self-expressive component many first-year students rely on (though I haven't entirely eliminated that type of assignment). This strategy is both theoretical and pedagogical. Some students (in any classroom) feel uncomfortable with writing exercises that ask them to examine and/or reveal themselves or their feelings about and reactions to the material. In the case of the essays in the text, that effect can be exacerbated by the sensitivity of the subject matter. The risk is that students will reject everything you've attempted to convey to them. Focusing on the structural aspects of the issues at hand rather than on personal reactions to those issues can alleviate some of this resistance. For this reason, you might downplay the expressive writing assignments but leave students room for figuring out their place within the social scheme.

Using Media in the Classroom

I chose to include a *Recommended Media* section in each part of the manual because I believe that students will benefit from actually *seeing* how the issues *Race, Class, and Gender in the United States*, seventh edition, brings up are represented. While by no means comprehensive, I've taken great care in choosing various types of media my colleagues or I have used or would want to use in our own classes. It is important to supplement Rothenberg's text with interdisciplinary materials. Thus, the media that have been chosen cover a range from documentaries, "serious" films, and popular movies to photographs, folk music, and Internet sites. The listings are meant as suggestions only, and some of them require that you do research in order to find the media sources in your area. You might also consider assigning a novel or other supplementary text or sending your students to museums or cultural events. When students experience these issues outside of the textbook proper, their own writing will improve since they will have more to write about and will feel even more engaged with the things Rothenberg's text brings up.

Using i>clicker in Your Class

There is a new section in this *Instructor's Resource Manual*—the Self-Assessment/i<clicker questions that follow the introductions to the parts of the text book. These questions are designed to allow instructors to take the temperature of their classes, either via in-class assessment activities or through the new i>clicker technology, an explanation of which follows.

What is i>clicker?

i>clicker (www.iclicker.com) is a new 2-way radio-frequency solution developed by a team of educators at the University of Illinois in partnership with Holtzbrinck Publishing Services (the parent company of Worth Publishers). Each step of i>clicker's development has been informed by teaching and learning research. We have developed content that works with the i>clicker (and, if you choose, other personal response) systems.

Why should faculty use a clicker/personal response system in a humanities and/or social science classroom setting? Because it:

A. encourages active engagement in the classroom

B. provides both instructors and students with real-time feedback

C. encourages reading prior to the class/lecture

D. encourages conceptual understanding (application-based) of the material

E. allows an instructor to take attendance

Response systems have become a meaningful solution in addressing the following classroom obstacles and objectives:

A. Improving the quality of the lecture. The traditional lecture is frequently anathema to learning; the student is anonymous and passive, and communication is often one-sided. Response systems remove, to a large degree, the anonymity of large sections and allow the instructor to better encourage student discussion and peer-to-peer interaction.

B. Providing immediate feedback to the instructor. In traditional lecture formats, instructors often misjudge student understanding of course material until the first exam. Classroom response systems enable instructors to discover instantly the level at which their students (collectively and individually) understand the lecture content. They can then adapt lectures based upon this feedback and improve overall learning.

C. Providing immediate feedback to the student and improving student learning outcomes. Students frequently mistake familiarity with course content for true comprehension . . . until the first exam. Response systems enable students to apply and test their knowledge (conceptually) to get a more accurate sense of their mastery of the course material. There is very little research on clickers and educational efficacy (most has been done by Eric Mazur and team at Harvard University). The most credible research recommends using response systems to engage students through two teaching practices: formative assessment and peer instruction.

   1. Formative assessment emphasizes mastery of course material (on a conceptual level) instead of evaluation of performance or assignment of grades (i.e., tests, high-points quizzes, or homework). The key to formative assessment is the role of feedback; this feedback allows students to correct conceptual errors and encourages instructors to modify their teaching according to what students know or don't know. Since formative assessments are designed to guide learning and are not used as an outcome measure, they are generally used as a low-stakes assessment (i.e., few points).

   2. Through peer instruction, learners help each other and learn by teaching. When students teach and learn from their fellow students, they are more engaged and more motivated to learn. Students are able to hear and consider alternate explanations. The best way to apply this approach to classroom response systems is to pose a conceptual question, pair students together and encourage discussion, and then ask them to vote. Research shows that this results in significant improvements in student-learning outcomes. In short, the more students talk to each other about a concept, the better their understanding of that concept.

D. Encouraging student preparation (i.e. reading prior to the lecture). "My students don't read the book and are poorly prepared for my class" is one of the most universal complaints among higher education faculty. As noted earlier, the use of classroom response systems to engage students is futile if students have not read the required material before class. A new journal study (in press) indicates that using a combination of online testing and clickers to require student participation improves the overall quality of discussions in lecture and overall course outcomes.

E. Managing attendance. Attendance policies are often difficult to impose in lecture settings; response systems offer an inexpensive and efficient system to enforce institution-wide attendance requirements.

F. Administering high-stakes, paperless exams and homework ("self-managed assessment"). While a select number of college professors find the high-stakes testing approach appealing, recent research and user testimonies reveals that using classroom response systems for high-stakes testing is risky, pedagogically ineffective, and difficult to administer. (Note that the i>clicker system is not configured for high-stakes or "self-managed" assessments, and is therefore not a good solution for teachers or professors seeking to use response systems in this way.)

How does our content work with i>clicker software?

i>clicker software works with any existing presentation or other software (Power-Point, Excel, Word, XML, Flash, Internet). There is no need to re-author questions or lectures into our software. Instead, the i>clicker bar floats on top of the course materials and presentation. The i >grader screen shot function captures your screen every time you begin polling. This feature offers you the opportunity to review their lecture and clicker questions after class without the drawback of having to re-author their questions in a complicated software application.

To learn more about i>clicker or to schedule a Web-based demonstration, contact your Worth Publishers representative or email i>clicker at sales@iclicker.com.

i>clicker system requirements

PC

    Windows XP Professional or Home Edition,

    or Windows XP Tablet PC Edition

    One USB port

    Projection system

    Screen Resolution of 1024 x 768

Macintosh

    Mac OS X

    One USB port

Final Thoughts

This manual is different from others because it does not have assignments to accompany every article in the book. Rather, each set of assignments has been designed to stimulate your own thinking and teaching and to encourage the flexible uses that are possible with this text. There is another important difference: It is my position that all texts (be they advertisements, essays, poems, films, or narrative fiction) convey *arguments*. In fact, the world views presented in materials that seem lacking in arguments are precisely those that can be most insidious because they are purportedly neutral. I highly recommend that you review and assign Rothenberg's introductory essays to each part in the book and the "Further Reading" selections at the end of each chapter. The introductions provide excellent overviews of the material, and the bibliographies give students a place to start for research projects or their own continuing studies.

A Note to Community College Instructors

Recently, I attended a talk given by the chancellor of the community college district where I work. The chancellor demonstrated by way of a pie chart the incredible diversity present in our schools. She called it a "rainbow pie," and indeed, that's exactly what it looked like. While my district sits smack in the middle of San Diego, and includes the most urban and ethnically diverse campus in the county, I couldn't help but think that this pie chart probably represented many, many other community colleges and districts. Thus, *Race, Class, and Gender in the United States*, seventh edition lends itself very well to use within a community college setting. With Rothenberg's emphasis on analysis of systemic issues, and her illumination of the ways we are all socially constructed by the society we live in, students in community college classrooms will find a great deal in the text that speaks to their own life experiences. While some might have trouble engaging with the essays' confrontation of social, cultural, and historical issues, many more will probably find that the material provides them with important tools for thinking about their own particular social contexts. The foregrounding of issues of economics and class, particularly, will speak to students in community colleges. Whether they are Latino, Latin American, African, African American, Asian, Asian American, Indian, Jewish, European American, Eastern European, Native American, white, black, brown, yellow, or red, students from all ethnicities and/or races will often find that they share certain affinities with regard to economic class. As so many students attend community colleges because of economic hardship, discussions of how their lives have been informed by such issues can be particularly fruitful in such a setting.

The textbook's collection of essays concerning *difference* and its construction will also speak to the diverse population a community college often serves. Students will respond to how the essays explore, rather than demonize, the manner in which race, class, gender, and sexuality are constructed in the United States. Often, they themselves, because of their own class background, ethnicity, race, gender, or sexuality (or combinations of these categories), have felt marginalized or left out of society. Many times students are attending community colleges in order to improve their lives and to acquire education or skills that will enable them to either transfer

9

to a four-year university or get a better job. A text such as *Race, Class, and Gender in the United States,* seventh edition can be useful for such students by helping them see that their particular place in American society is not a natural, inevitable phenomenon but, rather, a product of social and historical forces, and thus changeable. For students to realize that attitudes, ideas, and constructions of various modes of thinking are fluid and are products of historical processes can be enormously empowering—especially for people who might need support to continue on in their education and their new paths in life.

Such sensitivity to the struggles students are engaged in can make for a lively classroom and heated discussion. When students feel included, when texts speak to their experience of the world and give them tools or language to describe their place in society, they are actively engaged and bound to benefit from exposure to new ways of thinking. As I mentioned in the general introduction, students must also confront, rather than discount, concepts that might make them uncomfortable in this text. They need to learn how to think their way through difficult issues instead of merely dismissing them as "politically correct" or ignoring them altogether. This is why the assignments in this manual focus so much on facilitating critical thinking.

Specific Benefits to the Community College Student

The assignments in the manual can be particularly useful in a community college writing classroom as often a great deal of discussion goes into defining and exploring terms, ideas, and ways of looking at issues. Another aspect of this manual that will be useful for community college instructors is the emphasis on group work, small-group discussions, idea-generating assignments, and journal writing. The assignments provide ample space for exploration and definition of terms to give students the time they might need to really think through their perspectives and their ideas before beginning their writing process. Indeed, this manual is designed to encourage students to see the writing process as a continuum: from critical reading and thinking, to crafting an essay. Much as Rothenberg sees the essays in the text as engaging in nonoppositional thinking about issues of race, class, gender, and sexuality, this manual does the same sort of thing for class assignments. The process orientation of the manual lends itself well to the sort of teaching that goes on in a community college classroom where a great deal of work goes into helping students see reading and writing as useful and beneficial skills, and not as torturous, impossible tasks. By emphasizing process and idea formation, I hope to help community college instructors use *Race, Class, and Gender in the United States,* seventh edition, in their classrooms in the most effective ways possible.

Level of Language

Finally, a word about the language in the essays. This text contains a variety of voices, some very colloquial and others fairly theoretically sophisticated. As Rothenberg notes in *Race, Class, and Gender in the United States,* seventh edition, she deliberately chose readings that would speak to various reading levels. Many students may have trouble negotiating the language in the more difficult essays. In the manual, therefore, I have tried to focus students' attention on key terms in order to allow them to define such ideas for themselves. By drawing students' attention to the words that might give them the most trouble, the power of definition is placed squarely in their court. While some essays might not be appropriate for all levels of community college classes, instructors should feel confident that with a little extra work, the ideas for thinking and writing that the essays contain will lead to wonderfully complex and interesting learning and essay writing. Thus, for any community college course that contains either a critical thinking and/or a research component, Rothenberg's text offers challenging, useful, and important material to aid in such endeavors.

The Social Construction of Difference: Race, Class, Gender, and Sexuality

Part I delineates some of the many ways society forms human subjects and their attitudes toward themselves and others, as well as the ways differences between and among people are created and maintained. Through her selection of pieces, Rothenberg wants to draw attention to how differences occur and how hierarchies are established from such perceived differences. Beginning with discussions of race and ethnicity, Rothenberg then goes on to cover gender, sexuality, and class in her effort to denaturalize the very aspects of ourselves that we take to be the most "natural." Thus, the essays dealing with sexuality, for example, are often very interesting to students because they make them look at the ways the most personal parts of themselves are subject to social construction.

Self-Assessment/i>clicker Questions

- Do you consider yourself to have a "race"? A) Yes, B) No
- Have you ever been discriminated against? A) Yes, B) No
- Do you believe sexuality is: A) Determined by biology? or B) Determined by society and culture?
- Do you think heterosexuality is "natural"? A) Yes, B) No
- Do you think masculinity and femininity are "socially constructed"? A) Yes, B) No
- Do you think attitudes toward disabled people are "socially constructed"? A) Yes, B) No
- Do you think poor people are: A) That way because of their own problems? or B) That way because of systemic issues?

Issues and Questions to Consider

(The topics that appear under the heading "Issues and Questions to Consider" in each part are designed to help you initiate class discussions and clarify aspects of the readings that might be confusing or challenging for your students.)

- Part I establishes the themes that will be repeated throughout the volume. This is the time to emphasize to students the economic and historical basis for socially constructed categories. Race categories are born of economic conflict. Gender categories, likewise, function economically. When economics shift, so do these categories.

- Emphasize to your students the idea that social constructs are real—as evidenced by many of the essays in this section—in that they have effects. That is different, however, from saying that they are natural or inevitable. They are constructed, and there is historical evidence to prove it. As Judith Lorber puts it in "'Night to His Day': The Social Construction of Gender": "Whatever genes, hormones, and biological evolution contribute to human social institutions is materially as well as qualitatively transformed by social practices. Every social institution has a material base, but culture and social practices transform that base into something with qualitatively different patterns and constraints." You might discuss what she means by this.

- Many students want to see differences as necessary and useful defining characteristics of human beings. To discuss issues of race and ethnicity, gender, sexuality, and class as social constructs, with no inherently "natural" meanings, is often unsettling to students who may desperately want to emphasize differences between men and women or between other groups. Often, students feel that if differences are discussed and evaluated in class, they are being asked to eliminate them altogether—an impossibility in our current society. But as a point of departure for discussion, take a topic from Part I, such as race, and talk about what society would be like if no racial differences existed. What would such a society look like? Such an exercise is useful for making distinctions between the idea that no differences should exist and the idea that differences in this culture represent the ways various people are defined hierarchically depending on the color of their skin, their ethnic background, their gender, their sexuality, or their class. In other words, differences do exist, and the point is not necessarily that there shouldn't, for example, be any distinctions between men and women; rather, the ways each gender is *valued* in this culture can be extremely unfair and even dangerous. A useful way to end this discussion would be to bring in Jean Baker Miller's piece, "Domination and Subordination." Who is dominant? Who is subordinate? Why?

- In "The Ethics of Living Jim Crow," Richard Wright describes what it was like to grow up under laws and attitudes that assumed black people and white people were two different species, with whites being inherently more valuable than blacks. Although the laws were overturned during the civil rights struggles of the fifties and sixties, attitudes and ideologies are harder to deal with. Drawing on the work of Michael Omi and Howard Winant and Pem Davidson Buck, how have things changed? How are they the same? How does the history of slavery and Jim Crow affect the ways African American identities are socially constructed in our contemporary society? To what end?

- Ask students to consider questions of history. In current debates, recent immigrants—especially "illegal" ones—have been demonized by everyone from politicians and the mass media to people who have benefited from their labor. Karen Brodkin's piece provides an overview of the history and immigration patterns of Jews in America, and it offers a perspective on recent discussions of the "problems" of immigration. How do students view this history? How does it affect their understanding of contemporary approaches to immigration? What do they make of the fact that "white" groups were discriminated against in the past as "others"? How does an understanding of history facilitate one's analysis of current issues or problems?

- What are the multiple ways gender is socially constructed? What are the stereotypes surrounding femininity? Masculinity? What happens when someone does not fit these norms? What is the difference between "sex" and "gender"? (Lorber, Hubbard, Kimmel)

- What happens to one's view of sexuality when one does not see it as "natural"? How does that influence or change attitudes toward homosexuality or bisexuality, for example? If heterosexuality is a social construct, what about procreation? What role does biology play in the construction and maintenance of sexuality? What happens when one disconnects sexuality from gender? When one stops seeing men as inherently sexual and women as asexual or merely sexualized objects? (Hubbard, Katz, Kimmel)

- What happens to one's view of "disability" when one stops defining it as a "condition," but rather sees it, also, as being socially constructed? How has the language of disability permeated our culture to such an extent that it is used consciously and unconsciously to dismiss or denigrate the contributions of various constituencies in U.S. society? In what way does such language encourage or facilitate inequality, as Douglas Baynton puts it in his piece? And how are disabled people discounted by such language?

- In "Deconstructing the Underclass," Herbert Gans discusses how the public's perception of class is shaped by the terms we use to describe it. How are poor or working-class people viewed in this society? How is nature tied into conceptions of who belongs in what class? What are the pitfalls of thinking about this country as being either "classless" or as having a huge middle class to which everyone belongs?

Assignments

Generating Ideas/Small-Group Discussions

ASSIGNMENT 1. In almost all of the essays in Part I, race, gender, sexuality, and class are analyzed as, to use Omi and Winant's term, "pre-eminently sociohistorical concept[s]" (I, 1). That is, things "are given concrete expression by the specific social relations and historical context in which they are embedded." In your journal, take a page to discuss an aspect of race, gender, sexuality, or class as a "sociohistorical concept." How is your view of race or ethnicity different from the views held by people during the period Richard Wright describes in his piece "The Ethics of Living Jim Crow" (I, 2)? How are gender relations different now than in your parents' time? How does the current configuration of the government affect the way class is talked about? When you consider answers to these questions, avoid thinking in terms of "progress"—that is, that "things are better now than in the past." The point of addressing these questions in your journal is to get you thinking about social relations as inherently complicated processes that certainly change over time, but not always necessarily for the better.

ASSIGNMENT 2. At the beginning of "Racial Formations" (I, 1), Omi and Winant describe the case of Susie Guillory Phipps, who tried to sue the Louisiana Bureau of Vital Records in order "to change her racial classification from black to white." As the authors point out, this case brings to the fore questions concerning the definition of race and how people are racially marked. In a small group, discuss the ways each group member is "marked" racially. What, for example, is your whiteness composed of if that is how you define yourself? Your blackness? Your brownness? How is ethnicity "marked" in this culture? What are the implications of such marking for society? When you have spent several minutes on this task, spend a few more writing a page discussing what you learned about yourself and others. Evaluate yourself as a "raced" person. How do you fit into a culture that insists on marking its members?

ASSIGNMENT 3. Karen Brodkin (I, 4) describes her "surprise" that immigrant workers, such as Jews, were not always considered "white," since she grew up in a community that did not mark her as "ethnic." What do you make of her generational discussion of the ways immigrants became "white"? What does this essay say about whiteness? About the racialization of immigration? Why are contemporary immigrants seen as "dark," when many, in fact, are "white"?

ASSIGNMENT 4. On the chalkboard, your instructor will write down four categories: FEMALE/MALE, WOMAN/MAN. These are meant to make a distinction between categories of "sex" and "gender." Spend several minutes as a class listing the stereotypes or attributes of people under each category. What can you come up with? What do these stereotypes show about the ways people view sex and gender?

Are these categories set in stone? How are various attributes valued or devalued in our society? Why, do you think? Also think about how quickly you were able to come up with these stereotypes. What do you think this says about their staying power in this society? You can also do a similar exercise with class and ability: Divide the board up into four categories, POOR, WORKING CLASS, MIDDLE CLASS, UPPER CLASS, or into two categories, ABLED, DISABLED. How are these categories valued or devalued in this culture? What attributes are assigned to people in these categories? How did these attributes come into being, do you think?

ASSIGNMENT 5. In "The Invention of Heterosexuality" (I, 7), Jonathan Ned Katz not only highlights the ways heterosexuality is socially constructed but also historicizes the process by which such construction occurs. You may be challenged by Katz's assertion that one is not born a heterosexual but made one, which should lead to both lively discussions and interesting writing. After discussing the essay in class—and maybe pairing it with Lorber's (I, 5), Hubbard's "The Social Construction of Sexuality" (I, 6), and/or Kimmel's "Masculinity as Homophobia" (I, 8)—in your journal or as a homework assignment, write out a 1- to 2-page response/critique of Katz's article. What new ideas did you learn from the essay? Have you ever thought that something like sexuality could be socially constructed? In your own life, how have you noticed sexuality or gender as being constructed? How does homophobia function to regulate so-called "normal" sexual and gender identities? As a class, spend a week documenting ways that gender/sexuality is constructed. At the end of the week, reconvene and discuss everyone's findings as a class.

Writing Assignments

ASSIGNMENT 6: Read Jean Baker Miller's "Domination and Subordination" (I, 11) and consider the questions she poses at the beginning of the piece:
When does the engagement of difference stimulate the development and the enhancement of both parties to the engagement? And, conversely, when does such a confrontation with difference have negative effects: When does it lead to great difficulty, deterioration, and distortion and to some of the worst forms of degradation, terror, and violence—both for individuals and for groups—that human beings can experience?

Pick two hypothetical instances of what she describes and discuss them. When does one learn from encountering difference? And when does such an encounter lead to difficulty? Try to keep your essay focused on the institutional or systemic. You might look at issues surrounding bilingual education in schools, the history of mandatory or voluntary busing, women in the workplace, or the living-wage movement (to replace the minimum wage with the concept of a livable income).

ASSIGNMENT 7. Read "Racial Formations" (I, 1) and "The Ethics of Living Jim Crow" (I, 2), "Constructing Race, Creating White Privilege" (I, 3), and/or "How

Jews Became White Folks" (I, 4). How do Wright's, Buck's, and Brodkin's pieces illustrate what Omi and Winant are writing about? Focus your essay on two or three aspects where each piece echoes the other. For example, how does Wright describe his early process of "racialization" (Omi and Winant) as a boy living in Arkansas? How does Buck integrate discussions of laws regarding race and "race mixing" into her analysis of the construction of whiteness? What does Brodkin say about the linkage of whiteness and middle classness? How does Wright describe his racial consciousness as a "sociohistorical concept" (Omi and Winant)? Instead of the Wright, Buck, or Brodkin pieces, you can also use an article from Part VI and talk about how people from other ethnic groups undergo similar racializing processes.

ASSIGNMENT 8. Read Judith Lorber's "'Night to His Day': The Social Construction of Gender" (I, 5). Take a moment to think about the clothes you are wearing and the ways you dress yourself. How does Lorber's piece help you analyze the ways you construct yourself? How do clothing fashions aid in the social construction of gender? What does a woman or man say about herself or himself with various pieces of clothing? Write an essay in which you explore these issues.

Research/Analysis Projects

ASSIGNMENT 9. From your journal or homework assignments on Katz's "The Invention of Heterosexuality" (I, 7), look at a particular practice or phenomenon (homosexuality, heterosexuality, bisexuality, gendered fashions, particular words— "straight," "queer"—or phrases, behaviors, etc.) and formulate some sort of thesis statement or argument about it. How is this practice/phenomenon viewed by society? Why? What effect does this point of view have on the people who live their lives in this way? An interesting research project might be for you to look at a history of sexuality in America and examine a practice in a historical/contextual frame. If you are heterosexual, how did you come to act the way you do? What in the culture (films, ads, TV shows, books, Valentine's Day, etc.) presents a model for your way of being? In other words, place a contemporary sexual role or gendered behavior in the past in context, and talk about how the past construction impacts contemporary constructions of your topic.

ASSIGNMENT 10. Omi and Winant (I, 1) primarily discuss the social construction of African Americans as black, and what that construction has meant historically as well as currently. Take another group—Latinos, Asians, Native Americans, and so on—and do a similar analysis. Research the group's history in the United States. What were early constructions of this group's racial/ethnic attributes? How have people from several countries or regions been collapsed into one general category? (e.g., "Asians," which stands in for people who are from a wide range of places such as China, Japan, Korea, Thailand, India, Pakistan, and so). How does this impact the way these people are viewed by the dominant society? How does this lumping together erase essential differences between peoples' distinct cultures? What have these groups become in contemporary parlance? How are they constructed in everyday life by the media, the government, schools? Brodkin's "How Jews Became White Folks" (I, 4) or Buck's "Constructing Race, Creating White Privilege" (I, 3) would be useful essays to draw from here.

ASSIGNMENT 11. While reading Lorber's article (I, 5), pay close attention to her discussion of sports. You might also take a look at Kimmel's piece in this part (I, 8), and Sabo's and Jordan's pieces in Part VI. With the addition of the Women's National Basketball Association to professional spectator sports and the successes of women's soccer teams, how do male and female athletes compare? How are they constructed in the media? To do this project, you might survey several issues of sports magazines, such as *Sports Illustrated*, and watch several days of ESPN, Fox Sports, and the like. What do these mass-mediated outlets do in their constructions of femininity and masculinity? Of sexuality? Of race and ethnicity?

ASSIGNMENT 12. After reading Gans's article "Deconstructing the Underclass" (I, 10), research and discuss how poor people are portrayed in contemporary culture. You might want to reference the two articles by Gregory Mantsios (Parts II and VIII), in particular, "Media Magic: Making Class Invisible" (VIII, 7). Survey the news media or popular culture for ways that the poor are represented. How do such portrayals affect people's vision of the poor and of themselves? Are there any mass-media representations that do not fall into easy stereotyping? If so, what are they and how are their representations different from the norm? You might compare and contrast a couple of different constructions of the poor or working classes to illustrate your arguments.

ASSIGNMENT 13. After reading "Domination and Subordination" by Jean Baker Miller (I, 11), write an essay in which you analyze the concept of the "dominant group." You might also refer to Buck's (I, 3) and Brodkin's (I, 4) essays on whiteness, Katz's essay on heterosexuality (I, 7), Kimmel's piece on masculinity (I, 8), and Gans's article on class (I, 10). Perhaps incorporating some of Baynton's observations about the language of ability and disability (I, 9), you may want to ask, how does dominance operate in U.S. society? What happens when you make visible the dominant groups? Is it important to understand this concept? Why or why not? What can we gain from understanding how such dominance is constructed and maintained? Make sure to provide specific examples to illustrate your points.

Recommended Media

- Show Spike Lee's *Do the Right Thing*. What is "doing the right thing" for Lee's character? What do the race relations in this film show about the ways people construct each other through the lens of skin color? How do issues of class play out in the film? In other words, why does Lee's character keep working in the pizza parlor, even though he is treated as less than human at times?

- Show *American History X*, and discuss how the film deals with the making of a racist and the unmaking of one. Does the film work? Why or why not? What roles do class and masculinity play in the film? Does seeing a film about white supremacists make other forms of racism more or less visible? What effect does a film like this have on anti-racist projects?

- To interrogate issues of the "naturalness" of gender or sexuality, show *Paris is Burning* or *Wigstock*. How do these films foreground the constructedness of gender roles and/or sexuality? How do they contest the "naturalness" of femininity as attached to women and masculinity as attached to men?

- Show the "Malibu Stacy" episode of *The Simpsons*. Why does Lisa want to make her own talking Barbie-like doll? What does this episode say about how dolls contribute to gender role construction? With the class, you might also interrogate Grandpa Simpson's own journey. What is this episode doing with age and ageism?

- Show the film *My Left Foot*. Even though this film is set in Britain, how does the story of Christy Brown's life and how he dealt with his cerebral palsy illustrate Baynton's points about disability and the language of disability? The film reviews all laud Brown's "courage" and "determination" in dealing with his disability, yet he was also hard drinking and fairly clear-eyed in his approach to life. How is our society's penchant for defining disability as "lack" borne out in these reviews? How does this film challenge or uphold our definitions of disability?

Understanding Racism, Sexism, Heterosexism, and Class Privilege

The essays in Part I examine the concept of social construction and how it can help us see the ways systems of race, class, gender, and sexuality function to establish the boundaries of our lives. Rothenberg's selections in Part II aid in extending our understanding of how racism, sexism, heterosexism, and class privilege operate in extending power to some in this society but not to everyone. This part also maps out interconnections between the various systems in order to help students comprehend that these "isms" most often work together, overlap, and compound one another. The power of words, of definitions, of language itself is explored in this part's selections, and the essays invite students to consider the multiple ways they might participate in or be impacted by structures of domination. Rothenberg's selection of pieces foregrounds a structural analysis of power relations, and in her introduction she is careful to provide precise definitions for words such as "racism" and "sexism." The pieces here echo Rothenberg's concerns over the sense of these terms. While some students might balk at what they could see as the essays' too-narrow definition of "racism," "color blind racism," "internal racism," "sexism," "prejudice," "discrimination," and so on, such resistance should lead to lively conversations regarding the meaning and use of politically charged words. Thus, students will benefit from the authors' careful discussion of how they see racism, sexism, discrimination, prejudice, and privileges of all sorts operating in a range of situations.

Self-Assessment/i>clicker Questions

- Do you think racism exists? A) Yes, B) No

- Have you ever been affected by racism? A) Yes, B) No

- Do you think patriarchy exists? A) Yes, B) No

- Do you believe: A) Sexism exists to this day? B) Sexism is a thing of the past?
- Is heterosexuality the norm? A) Yes, B) No
- Are whites privileged in the United States? A) Yes, B) No
- Does your class position affect your opportunities? A) Yes, B) No

Issues and Questions to Consider

- Before discussing the essays in this section, ask students for their definitions of the term "political correctness." You may be surprised at some of the answers you get. You might then devote a moment to outlining the history of this term (that it started in left-leaning circles in the sixties to chide someone for being too dogmatic, and that it was picked up by the right in the eighties and nineties to put the brakes on "overly sensitive" speech which, as pundits and politicians saw it, was a result of multicultural education run amok). What are the implications of this term? Can one ever be "too" politically correct? Why or why not? Why might we want to be careful about the way we say or define things?

- Spend time considering the different definitions of "racism" this part explores. Rothenberg, Bonilla-Silva, Osajima, Tatum, Sethi, and McIntosh all discuss this term, and all have somewhat different understandings of the word. Which definition seems to be the most accurate? Why?

- Both Johnson is a male writer considering the concepts of sexism and patriarchy. Discuss with students what they think of men writing about sexism, whites writing about white privilege and racism, heterosexuals writing about homophobia and heterosexism, and middle-class people writing about the poor. In Part VIII, Ayvazian analyzes the concept of "allies." How do some of the authors in Part II model such a concept?

- Spend some time discussing Frye's image of the birdcage. Why is this a useful image for describing oppression? How might you use the image to describe other issues such as racism or class discrimination? Many students have trouble with Frye's door opening discussion. They might believe she "makes too big a deal out of it," that "men are just being nice," and that "I [i.e., women] do it, too—is that bad?" You will probably have to outline how this is an example of a bar in the birdcage very specifically for them.

- In Part I we discussed the social construction of race, gender, sexuality, and class, and the ways these subject positions are designed so different attributes have differing values. In this part, we are looking at the ways attributes such as race, gender, sexuality, and class are valued negatively, and we are learning how to describe them in order to contest such negative evaluations. Explore with students how such negative evaluations might have come into being. This would be an ideal time to bring in

Osajima's essay to outline how prejudice operates psychologically and internally. You might also discuss why systems of domination must be religiously policed. Why, for example, if dominant groups so firmly hold power, does there need to be a system of language that enforces the oppression of others? Could it be that dominant groups are not "naturally" better than others but are so by virtue of their skin color, their gender, their sexuality, and/or their class position? In other words, must a system of domination uphold itself in order to distract people from its social construction? Look also at Tatum's and Pharr's pieces to explore these issues.

- Some of the essays discuss internalized racism, sexism, or class privilege. How does this happen? What is the result of such thinking? What might be effective ways of combating this kind of thinking?

- Sethi's and Osajima's articles detail conflicts among and within "ethnic" populations. Both authors explore the manner in which various groups discriminate against each other and among each other, and both authors also try to expand discussions of race and ethnicity beyond a black-white paradigm. How do these discussions help students visualize a more complex society? How might the complication of these issues aid students in analyzing the operation of structures of domination? In particular, regarding prejudices among various people that can be traced to media representations (say, of Koreans toward African Americans), how might such sentiments defamiliarize, or make unfamiliar, the very act of stereotyping that occurs daily in this country? You might also choose some readings from Part III to flesh out this discussion.

- Many white students might feel uncomfortable with McIntosh's discussion of white privilege. Explore with the class what it means to make whiteness "visible" as a racial category in order to analyze it. How is whiteness rendered "invisible" through ideology, and to what effect?

Assignments

Generating Ideas/Small-Group Discussions

ASSIGNMENT 1. Your instructor will split the class up into small groups of about four to five people and then write some terms and "isms" (discrimination, prejudice, ideology, racism, sexism, homophobia, heterosexism, classism or class privilege, ableism, ageism, etc.) on the board. After being assigned a term or "ism," each group should define its assigned concept and then come up with a specific example of how the concept operates in everyday life. Each group should then present its findings to the rest of the class in order to begin a discussion of its particular concept.

ASSIGNMENT 2. In Peggy McIntosh's "White Privilege: Unpacking the Invisible Knapsack" (II, 8), readers are confronted by the ways whiteness is made to seem "normal" in the United States. Often it has never occurred to many so-called white people how they can be privileged by virtue of their skin color—even though whiteness is always visible to nonwhite people. In a group or individually, identify some way in which you're "privileged"—that is, by class, by gender, by education, by being part of a tightly knit community, or some other way. How does this privilege manifest itself? Have you ever thought you were privileged in this way? What are your assumptions about others who do not share this privilege? Discuss your explorations with the rest of the class.

ASSIGNMENT 3. In your journal, discuss the connections you can make between Marilyn Frye's birdcage (II, 5), Beverley Daniels Tatum's analysis of "internalized oppression" (II, 1), and Keith Osajima's discussion of "internalized racism" (II, 3). What do these three ideas have in common? How does the birdcage illustrate Osajima's point about Asian Americans often "see[ing] and defin[ing] themselves in relation to the images and stereotypes circulating in the dominant society"? Or Tatum's idea that members of oppressed groups often "[believe] the distorted messages about one's own group"? What specific examples can you come up with that describe the bars of the cage?

ASSIGNMENT 4. Read the essay by Pharr (II, 7), who argues that homophobia is a debilitating aspect of the culture that affects us all. Did Pharr's essay make you uncomfortable, or did you find yourself agreeing with her position? In your journal, describe your reactions to this essay. Isolate specific moments in the piece that troubled you. What portions of the essay did you admire? In class, discuss this essay and link it up with Johnson's (II, 6) and Frye's (II, 5) pieces. How do homophobia and sexism work as mechanisms of social control?

ASSIGNMENT 5. Spend some time in a small group discussing class. Before group members share their personal class histories, they should review Mantsios's "Class in America" (II, 9) in order to clarify their terminology. Individually, members should identify where they stand with regard to class and why they've chosen to position themselves there. Finally, they should ask themselves why it's important to understand one's class position. How does this help you understand class in America and class discrimination?

ASSIGNMENT 6. In a pair, follow Gregory Mantsios's (II, 9) model of a hypothetical person, construct identities for yourselves, and interview each other. (What is your class, race, gender, educational background, and so on?) After constructing your persons, make some predictions among yourselves about their futures. Will each be a "success"? Why or why not? How does Mantsios's outlining of myths/realities of class help you see what goes into determining a person's future?

ASSIGNMENT 7. After reading Eduardo Bonilla-Silva's essay "Color-blind Racism" (II, 2), think about a time you might have expressed some prejudice toward others, and write about it in your journal. Did you express this bias overtly? How? How did you feel about it at the time? Later? Write 1-2 pages on this experience.

Writing Assignments

ASSIGNMENT 8. Take one of the key terms from Part II—racism, sexism, hetero-sexism, homophobia, oppression, discrimination, prejudice, class discrimination, and so on—and analyze it. If your class has done the "isms" exercise, you might choose a term that your group did *not* investigate—or you might extend your group's findings. Use at least two articles from this part that deal with the term in some way. You might choose to address Rothenberg's concerns in her introduction to Part II in your paper. Do you think a more precise definition of your term is necessary? Or do you think it should be broadened? How do you see your term operating in society? Feel free to draw on a personal narrative from Part V to show how you see your term operating in American society. How would you alter how people are socially constructed in order to eliminate your term? What solutions can you offer to see this happen?

ASSIGNMENT 9. Read a real-life news story from Part IV or a personal narrative from another part (Alsutany, Wu, Cofer, Wright, or Terkel would all be good) in order to look at the ways McIntosh's observations about privilege or lack of privilege play out in someone's life (II, 8). What have you learned from looking at things from this perspective? How do you view your own life, your own experiences? What personal experiences make you think about race and/or ethnicity? About whiteness? Make sure, however, that you tie your own experience into larger, systemic issues. You might also draw on the report by the U.S. Commission on Civil Rights in order to structure your essay (IV, 1).

ASSIGNMENT 10. Discuss a birdcage you inhabit or might inhabit (II, 5). What makes up its bars? What structures in society close you in, keep you from having access to the best life you could lead? Or, instead, create a narrative about someone else's birdcage. Try to put yourself in someone else's shoes for a moment, and describe what sorts of bars keep him or her in place. Construct someone who is totally different from you, but make sure that you pay attention and are sensitive to the multiple ways the person's life may diverge from your own. What is his or her ethnicity or race? Gender? Class standing? Occupation? Educational level? Does she or he live in a rural area or an urban one? Is the person in a relationship? What is his or her sexual orientation? And so on. All of these things will affect your construction of that person's or your own birdcage.

Research/Analysis Projects

ASSIGNMENT 11. Read Rita Chaudhry Sethi's essay "Smells Like Racism" (II, 4) carefully and write an essay on a particular ethnic group. How has this group been stereotyped in American society? Why, do you think? How has it been constructed as "other"? In your essay, be sure to research your group so you can discuss how certain practices are misunderstood by other people in the dominant culture. What is the history of your group in America? What sorts of examples can you come up with about the ways this group has been dealt with in popular culture, indeed, in the culture at large? How is this group perceived by other minority and/or immigrant groups? Why is this so, do you think? Maybe go to the U.S. Census website (www.census.gov) and look at some statistics of your group. Use several sources so that you can do as thorough a job as possible.

ASSIGNMENT 12. After reading Eduardo Bonilla-Silva's essay, "Color-Blind Racism" (II, 2) carefully, design an interview project that models his own. Select a cohort of people, design some interview questions surrounding race and racism, and code your results following Bonilla-Silva's categories. Are your results similar or different? What could account for the differences? What type of cohort did you interview? What part of the country were you in? Were you in a city or a rural area? What were your subjects' races, ethnicities, gender, socioeconomic classes? Etc. What insights did you gain from doing this project?

ASSIGNMENT 13. Research some of the articles on "internalized racism" (Osajima, II, 3). How pervasive is it? How does it operate in our society? Make sure you provide specific examples as well as documentation for your discussion.

ASSIGNMENT 14. Research the history behind a gendered behavior, such as women wearing make-up or men watching sports, as Frye does with door opening (II, 5). Where does this behavior come from? What does it say about the construction of women and men? Can such behaviors ever just be "being nice" or "pretty" or "entertainment"? Why or why not?

Recommended Media

- Show *Thelma and Louise*, and discuss it in relation to Frye's birdcage. What are Thelma and Louise running away from? Why do they choose death rather than "going back"? What would they be "going back" to? You might also ask your class how their whiteness and heterosexuality combine with their gender. Would this film be different if it were about two women of color or two lesbians on the lam from the police and the patriarchal state?

- You might show either *Falling Down* or *Blue Collar* to address issues of white middle-class or white working-class masculinity and oppressive economic structures. *Falling Down* would also illustrate some of the points Rita Sethi makes in her article about the film and its representation of "otherness."

- Show John Singleton's film, *Rosewood*. How does it illustrate all levels of discrimination? How, in fact, does it demonstrate that the term "discrimination" is often not strong enough and cannot stand in for "racism," for instance? What does Singleton's use of history add in drawing out these issues?

- Show the documentary *Hoop Dreams* and discuss the ways the film deals with the intersections of race and class.

Beyond Black and White: Complicating Questions of Race and Ethnicity

When one looks around the United States these days, one sees people of many different hues. In Part III, Rothenberg contests the continual reduction of racial and ethnic discussions to a black-white paradigm. The selections here highlight the ways immigration has and is going to completely alter the complexion of the United States. Many of the pieces, therefore, call for new paradigms to understand the rapidly-changing population in this country. Perhaps most surprising to some students will be the essays discussing the complicated relationships between races—Latinos and blacks, for example—and among people who fall under the same racial categories—Southeast Asian immigrants versus other Asians; "White Hispanics" versus "Black Hispanics"; etc. Rothenberg's careful selection of texts demonstrates the ways that the U.S. landscape is in constant flux. And while many issues of class and identity remain somewhat constant, we must continually reframe, reexamine, and rework our analytical framework to account for such diversity. Students will benefit from this more nuanced view of racial and ethnic issues in the United States.

Self-Assessment/i>clicker Questions

- Do you have friends of various ethnicities? A) Yes, B) No
- Do you think a more diverse United States is: A) A positive thing? B) A negative thing?
- Do you think that census figures on race and ethnicity are useful tools? A) Yes, B) No
- Is it important to know what a person's race or ethnicity is? A) Yes, B) No
- Do you think whites are still privileged in the United States? A) Yes, B) No

- Would you categorize your race or ethnicity? A) Yes, B) No
- Do you think immigration is: A) Good for a country? B) Bad for a country?
- Are you an immigrant? A) Yes, B) No

Issues and Questions to Consider

- Before discussing the essays in this section, have students voice their views on immigration, race, and ethnicity. How are these three categories interrelated in people's minds? Do they think immigration is a good thing? What about borders? What's their family background? Is it important for the census to measure race and ethnicity? Why or why not? Many students may have been exposed to ideas through the media, family, friends, etc., that hearing about race and ethnicity "too much" actually *causes* racial discrimination. You might have students review Bonilla-Silva's discussion of "color-blind racism" to challenge these notions.

- How do students themselves experience their day-to-day lives? If you have a diverse group, try to get them talking about the ways they view themselves and others. Do they believe there's been a "black-white paradigm" for understanding racial relations? How have they discussed these issues in other academic settings? How do they see these issues playing out in their own lives?

- Discuss with students the terms "race" and "ethnicity." What is the difference between these two terms? Have them refer specifically to both Navarro's and Tafoya's pieces. What, for example, is a "Black Hispanic"? What are the implications of such a racial/ethnic categorization?

- How do economics play out in these issues? Refer students to Thrupkaew's insights about people in Southeast Asian communities. You might also have students wrestle with Ching's assertion that race always trumps class. Does it?

Assignments

Generating Ideas/Small-Group Discussions

ASSIGNMENT 1. In your journal, describe, as best you can, your ethnicity. Were your ancestors immigrants? Where did they come from? Is your identity composed of more than one ethnicity? What cultural practices or traditions do you follow? Write 1–2 pages, and when you're finished, trade papers with another student. How were you two similar? Different? What did you learn from this? You might look back over Alsutany's essay "Los Intersticios: Recasting Moving Selves" (III, 3) before doing this assignment.

ASSIGNMENT 2. In a small group of 4-5 students, discuss what each of your answers would be to the race/ethnicity portion of the census. How does your group's answers compare to the findings in "Census Bureau Predicts Diverse U.S. Future" (III, 1)? What do you make of this?

ASSIGNMENT 3. Recently, immigrants' rights have been in the news with major protests in cities across the United States. Many immigrants' rights activists have come from Latino communities, and a lot of recent issues have stemmed from governmental attempts to not only reform immigration laws, but also to beef up security along the U.S./Mexico border in states such as Texas, Arizona, and California. In a small group, discuss the idea of "borders." What are they? What is their purpose? In a country such as the United States, which was founded by immigrants, why do we have borders? Choose a note-taker to record your conversation so you can make a report of what your group discussed to the rest of the class.

ASSIGNMENT 4. For homework, write 1–2 pages about the relationship between whiteness and being an American. Review Rubin's piece "Is This a White Country or What?" (III, 10) before starting this assignment. Why do you think being an American is often associated with being white?

Writing Assignments

ASSIGNMENT 5. After reading "Census Bureau Predicts Diverse U.S. Future" by Genaro C. Armas (III, 1) and "A New Century: Immigration and the U.S." by the MPI Staff (III, 2), write an essay in which you discuss the implications of the recent waves of immigration. Do these waves make the United States stronger and better? Weaker and worse? Somewhere in between?

ASSIGNMENT 6. In an essay, examine the ways race and ethnicity intersect. Look at Navarro's "Going Beyond Black and White, Hispanics in Census Pick 'Other'" (III, 4) and Tafoya's "Shades of Belonging: Latinos and Racial Identity" (III, 5) before starting your paper. Both these pieces deal with the conundrum many Latinos face when they are asked to identify themselves. Do they foreground their ethnicity? If so, what race do they put down on forms? Finally, what is the point of such hair splitting? Is gathering this information on people important? Why or why not? You might refer back to the Omi and Winant piece in Part I that starts the book.

ASSIGNMENT 7. Read "Asian American" by Sonia Shah (III, 6) and "The Myth of the Model Minority" (III, 7) by Noy Thrupkaew. In an essay, analyze some of the stereotypes about Asian Americans. On the one hand, following some of Thrupkaew's observations, what are some traditional stereotypes associated with Asian people? Where did they come from, do you think? On the other, why are Asian Americans also termed the "model minority"? What does Shah mean when she states: "While an education can be had and a living made based on model minority myths (at least for some), it is at the cost of indulging the racist delusion that there can be some 'good minorities' in implicit contrast to those other 'bad minorities,' who have only themselves to blame"? You might also look at "Goodbye Pat Morita, Best Supporting Asian" (IV, 14), which is a bittersweet homage to the Japanese American actor, Pat Morita, or Janice Mirikitani's poem, "Suicide Note" (VI, 6), which is written from the perspective of a young woman who kills herself because she doesn't achieve a perfect academic record. Mirikitani outlines, then, the brutality inherent in the "model minority" stereotype when someone internalizes its oppressive implications. What consequences do all of these depictions have for Asian Americans and for their relationships with other ethnic groups?

ASSIGNMENT 8. In "Facing Up to Race," Carrie Ching (III, 11) argues that: It's too easy to claim solidarity with people of different backgrounds from afar—you don't have to take chances and endure the discomfort of having your own perspective and your unconscious assumptions about race challenged. Examining and breaking down the racial boundaries in our personal lives are just as important as addressing injustices on a global scale.

Ching is primarily discussing the ways liberal whites will support refugees in other countries, but overlook injustice on our own shores. However, given the ways Part III outlines an extremely diverse U.S. population and discusses various conflicts between ethnic groups, how could you extend Ching's call to others? How do groups within the United States contribute to injustice toward others? How could these issues be solved? Take some of Ching's points and really explore the implications of her argument in your essay.

Research/Analysis Assignments

ASSIGNMENT 9. Do some research on the recent immigrants' rights protests around the country and write a paper in which you discuss your findings. You could focus on protests that took place in your community, or do a broader survey from across the United States What were people protesting? What kinds of "immigration reforms" has Congress been working on? What do you make of all of this? Did you attend any of the protests? What was your experience? You might consider interviewing an organizer and/or a participant in some of the protests to flesh out your essay. Did the protests accomplish what the organizers set out to do? How or how not?

ASSIGNMENT 10. Research the relationship between two ethnic groups in this country and write a paper about it. Make sure you look at Tilove's (III, 8) and Hutchinson's (III, 9) articles in this part to help you do this. What is the relationship between your two groups? What is their history with each other? How have cultural stereotypes of each group affected the ways they deal with each other? How can people begin to overcome dangerous and unhealthy stereotypes about each other? How can new constructions of various groups and various people be instituted in this society?

ASSIGNMENT 11. After reading Noy Thrupkaew's piece "The Myth of the Model Minority" (III, 7), research an ethnic or racial category and unpack it as Thrupkaew does with the term "Asian." What groups make up the term "Hispanic" or "African American," for example? How do the groups within that category break down into class divisions? Regional divisions? Country of origin? Write an essay that reveals who your umbrella term covers and discuss in ways that are similar to Thrupkaew's text how stereotypes about your term erase the various life experiences of the people that term is supposed to cover.

ASSIGNMENT 12. In Lillian Rubin's essay, "Is this a White Country or What?" (III, 10), she interviews several people who fear recent waves of immigration for economic reasons. As whites, too, they feel threatened by people claiming an ethnic identity since whiteness is such an amorphous construct. In an essay, research a "white" ethnicity such as Irish, Italian, Russian, Jewish, etc. Consult some of the other readings in the text that deal with whiteness (e.g., Buck and Brodkin in Part I) and look up historians' accounts of the construction of whiteness to flesh out your discussion. Was the ethnicity of your choice always in a privileged position? If not, how did your ethnicity become privileged? What can history help us understand about the current context regarding race and ethnicity in the United States?

Recommended Media

- Show the film *Crash* (2005) and discuss the ways the film uses a diverse group of characters to tell its story. What part does race and ethnicity play in developing the story? How does this film echo the readings in this section?

- Have students watch non-English, nonwhite television if they have cable, or tape a *telenovela* or a newscast from a Latino TV station or a show from an Asian TV station. The fact that these sorts of media are readily available nation-wide attests to just how diverse the United States has become. What can students learn from watching media produced by and for immigrants?

- Show the film *A Day Without a Mexican* (2004). What points does the film make about the U.S.'s reliance on immigrant labor? On Latinos? What would the United States lose if suddenly an entire ethnicity just disappeared? Have students consider these questions after watching this film.

- Another film that captures Latino life in Los Angeles and also deals with gender issues is *Real Women Have Curves*. This film is set in a small, downtown garment factory and shows the lives of the women who make the clothes we wear. Students will identify with the funny, down-to-earth young protagonist as she navigates the divide between generations and negotiates her place as a Chicana in the United States.

- For an interesting and hilarious collision of ethnicity, sexuality, and gender roles, show *The Wedding Banquet* (1993). Have students discuss the ways these identities intersect in this film about a Taiwanese man in a long-term gay relationship who has to get married to a woman for a green card.

- You might have students bring in a piece of music that they feel mixes perspectives or crosses ethnic boundaries—Latino rap music, Asian pop, etc. How does their music represent the extremely diverse culture in which we live?

Discrimination in Everyday Life

Part IV, composed of recent articles taken directly out of newspapers, magazines and Web sources, attempts to address students' desire to dismiss issues of race, class, gender, and sexuality as problems of the past. After grappling with complex terms and coming to some understanding of how ideology operates in American society, many students feel overwhelmed. The essays in Part IV ground the previous explorations of oppression, prejudice, discrimination, and so on, in real-life experience. When students read about a group of minority and women workers discriminated against when trying to get jobs at Abercrombie and Fitch, or a Muslim football player kicked off his team because of his religion, or a young lesbian drummed out of high school, issues of racism, religious intolerance, homophobia, and the like, are made concrete. Students are then able to go on and discover for themselves how facing such inequalities is a day-to-day occurrence for many people in this society. Part IV also provides a fine introduction to the personal narratives of Part VI. For courses that have a research component, this section gives students a great deal of material that they can use as examples in their own work. Part IV also provides a wide range of sources for them to use to support their arguments in their writing projects.

Self-Assessment/i>clicker Questions

- Do you believe that racism is largely a thing of the past? A) Yes, B) No
- Do you believe that gender discrimination: A) still exists, or B) is a thing of the past?
- Are there companies who don't want to hire people of color? A) Yes, B) No
- Is racial profiling: A) Never necessary; B) Sometimes necessary; C) Often necessary
- Is it important to strive for a "color-blind" society? A) Yes, B) No
- Should people be compelled to speak only English at work? A) Yes, B) No
- Have you ever been discriminated against on the basis of: A) race; B) ethnicity; C) gender; D) sexual orientation; E) class?
- Do you think the media presents a male-dominated world view? A) Yes, B) No

Issues and Questions to Consider

- Before discussing individual essays, spend some time with your class answering Rothenberg's question in her introduction: "Why . . . do so many people, in particular, so many young people, seem to believe that racism and sexism are largely things of the past?" Do or did your students feel this way? Why? Why is it easier to think this way than to see discrimination as an ongoing problem facing Americans? Have your students' feelings changed since doing the reading in this part? How?

- "The Problem: Discrimination," a 1981 report, usefully outlines three levels of discrimination in the United States. Spend time with students discussing the definitions of these levels. Does this piece help students map out the ways discrimination functions structurally and systemically in American society? How?

- Devote some time talking about the differences between intentional and unintentional racism, sexism, homophobia, and so on. What constitutes intentional? What constitutes unintentional? Are people who commit unintentional acts off the hook? Why or why not? How do people become aware of their own biases and try to address them in order to avoid committing hurtful acts of prejudice?

- Is striving for a "color-blind" or "gender-neutral" society the solution for the problems outlined in Part IV? Why or why not? What do both those terms imply? Do they eliminate racism and sexism? Or do they side-step racism and sexism? What other solutions might there be for dealing with institutional and individual discriminatory practices and attitudes?

- Have students read the newspaper or watch or listen to the news every day to monitor acts of discrimination. What do they see or hear when they do this? Ask them not only to read about and/or watch for incidents but also to pay attention to *how* the stories are written or reported on. Remind them that the media is another institution that has potential for discrimination built into it. What are journalists' assumptions and biases when they report a story? What is their world view, their own ideological perspective? Whose side do they seem to be on?

Assignments

Generating Ideas/Small-Group Discussions

ASSIGNMENT 1. "The Problem: Discrimination," a 1981 report by the U.S. Commission on Civil Rights, outlines three systemic levels of discriminatory practices — individual, organizational, and structural (IV, 1). By breaking discrimination into three levels, the report's authors are trying to make distinctions between various practices and also to complicate events to avoid any sort of easy answers. Your instructor will split the class up into several small groups; with your group members, discuss one of the examples in the article from the perspective of its three levels.

Next, choose an article from Part IV that will lend itself to this sort of systemic analysis. Reconvene with the rest of the class and discuss your examples.

ASSIGNMENT 2. For homework, write 1–2 pages in which you discuss how a piece in Part IV either did or did not help you visualize one of the concepts explored in Parts I, II, and III. How do real-life examples aid people in understanding the ways various forms of oppression manifest themselves? How does the event or situation in your article illustrate the ways socially constructed identities can be harmful?

ASSIGNMENT 3. Your instructor will break the class into small groups. Each group will choose a reading from Part IV and, using a concept or term from Part II, discuss what form or forms of discrimination the incident in the reading manifests. Group members should also talk about what interested them particularly about the reading—why did they choose it? Each group should present its discussion to the rest of the class.

ASSIGNMENT 4. As a class, using "The Problem: Discrimination" (IV, 1), categorize the readings in Part IV to understand how patterns of discrimination operate in this society. Why, for example, do you think there are several articles about hate crimes and stereotyping? Or about discriminatory hiring practices? Or about financial inequalities? How does power operate in and through institutions?

Writing Assignments

ASSIGNMENT 5. Read "Abercrombie Settles Class Action Suit" (IV, 2) and think about the clothing stores you frequent. Who are the sales clerks? Who are the stock people? You might take a trip to the mall and observe several stores. Write an essay in which you report your findings. Do you think suits like the one waged against Abercrombie and Fitch are warranted? Why or why not?

ASSIGNMENT 6. After reading "The Segregated Classrooms of a Proudly Diverse School" (IV, 19) and "College Choices are Limited for Students from Needy Families" (IV, 20), write about the implications of a built-in disparity among children in American schools. Analyze the article and perhaps draw on current discussions concerning school reform, such as vouchers, charter schools, magnet schools, resegregation or desegregation and the like. Do you think such programs will work? Why or why not?

ASSIGNMENT 7. Several of the articles in Part IV reveal rampant sexism, sexual harassment, and racial discrimination at some of the United States' most revered businesses—like Abercrombie and Fitch, L'Oreal, and Best Buy. These businesses often rely on low-wage workers to run their operations. What do you make of such hostile work environments? Write a paper in which you first outline the causes of such discriminatory practices, the practices themselves, and some possible solutions. Could the nature of the work foster such behavior? Why or why not, do you think?

ASSIGNMENT 8. The articles in Part IV all deal with discrimination that affects the most central aspects of peoples' lives: mobility, work, sexuality, education, finances, home, religion, safety, and the like. If you were going into a helping profession such as social work, counseling, nursing, or teaching, how does being aware of the pervasive aspects of discrimination help you in thinking about the people you will be dealing with? What insights can you glean from doing the readings in this part of the text? Make sure to cite some specific examples from the articles to support your exploration.

Research/Analysis Projects

ASSIGNMENT 9. Research the history of the term "civil rights" and analyze it. What does the term mean? What does it have to do with a democratic society? Make sure to cite specific examples to illustrate your points.

ASSIGNMENT 10. After reading the articles in Part IV, you are probably becoming more aware of how pervasive discrimination of all kinds is in our society today. Taking Part IV as a jumping-off point, research and analyze a story about some form of discrimination that happened recently. You may choose to focus on a local event or one that was reported nationally (like hate crimes against Muslims in the wake of 9/11, which you can also refer to in the article "Muslim Running Back Off the Team at New Mexico State," or something surrounding the response to Hurricane Katrina, etc.). In your paper, make sure to note not just what happened and what you think it means but also how the story was reported.

ASSIGNMENT 11. The article "Where 'English Only' Falls Short" by Stacy Teicher (IV, 5) details some of the issues non–native English speakers, including Navajos, confront when working in a place of business that requires that they speak only English. In an essay, first present some research on how often it is that employers make their workers speak only English. Then analyze your findings. Do you think it's appropriate for employers to dictate what language their employees use with each other? Why or why not?

ASSIGNMENT 12. Research an issue regarding affirmative action. In the last several years, citizens in some states, such as California, have voted in mandates to end affirmative action on the state and local levels. Schools, such as the University of Texas, have eliminated affirmative action admissions policies. In these cases, the justification for the actions was that affirmative action no longer worked. At the same time, the University of Michigan's law school was under attack, by President

George W. Bush no less, for holding onto its admissions policies that look at race and ethnicity as an enhancement for admittance to its school. Do you think affirmative action is still necessary? Why or why not, in your view? What does your research show? What do the articles in Part IV demonstrate? Is the "playing field" now "leveled" enough to give equal access to well-paying jobs and educational opportunities to women and minorities? Why or why not? Be sure to carefully document your sources and to draw from a variety of well-researched perspectives.

ASSIGNMENT 13. While several of the articles in Part IV focus on class inequities, especially as they intersect with race and gender, a few show that even if one is middle or upper class, inequities with regard to gender still exist. After reading the articles "Manhattan Store Owner Accused of Underpaying and Sexually Harassing Workers" by Steven Greenhouse (IV, 8) and "Show Me the Clout" by Sheila Gibbons (IV, 29), apparently about two very different situations, analyze the pervasive aspects of gender discrimination from top to bottom. Do some research on recent statistics to support your discussion. How far have women come? Has there recently been retrenchment with regard to equality? Why? Why might immigrant women or women of color be more vulnerable to economic injustice than others?

ASSIGNMENT 14. How does the media contribute to the maintenance of inequalities? Pick a category such as race, class, gender, sexuality, etc., and analyze how television deals with it. Survey recent TV shows—sitcoms, dramas, news shows—and collect data on the ways the media represents these categories. You might look at Sheila Gibbons's article on women in the news media (IV, 29) or Lynn Elber's study on Latinos in the news (IV, 28) for guidance on this project.

Recommended Media

- CBS, ABC, and NBC news shows have all done various stories documenting day-to-day racial discrimination. You might consult the networks' Web sites to find videotapes of those shows.

- Most of the stories in Part IV are from newspaper and magazine articles. Survey a couple of newspapers and magazines, or have your students pay attention to media sources, to bring in more stories to class. This will keep the material constantly up to date; at the same time, it will show that the stories in this part do not represent isolated incidents but, rather, ongoing problems.

- In class, you might go over your school's code of conduct and sexual harassment policies. Why are these regulations in place? What do they demonstrate to students about what the climate was for nonprivileged people in the past?

- Compare and contrast the ways race, ethnicity, gender, sexuality, class, bias, discrimination, etc., are reported on Fox News or MSNBC to the way they are reported in the pieces in Part IV. Videotape segments off of these channels and bring them in for your class to analyze. How do the frameworks of these networks impact the way they deliver information?

- Have your students check out an alternative news website such as www.cursor.org, AlterNet, or ZNet. You might also have them look at Fairness and Accuracy In Reporting's website (www.fair.org) and newsletter. These sources generally have a vastly different take on important news items from the major news media. Have students compare and contrast these sources.

The Economics of Race, Class, and Gender in the United States

In Part V, Rothenberg details the ways economics intersects with race, ethnicity, and gender to determine how people will be able to live their lives. Countering notions that poor people are poor because they are "naturally" less able, the essays in this part outline quite specifically recent economic trends that impact middle-class, working-class, working-poor, and poor peoples' lives in a myriad of ways. The essays here discuss how economic standing can affect the most basic aspects of our lives: relationships with each other, health, access to education, feelings of self-worth, and the ways we raise our children. When one factors in race or gender issues, these aspects can be significantly altered. For example, people of color who have attained middle-class standing might still be segregated in low-income neighborhoods because of the color of their skin, and women of all races who need public assistance are time and time again stigmatized as lazy, slovenly, and ignorant (although the combination of gender and race in discussions of welfare create truly racist and oppressive stereotypes). These essays will be helpful for students in that they present a wealth of information, both statistical and personal. The mix of well-researched data and narratives about personal economic experiences prevents students from dismissing these issues as mere "opinion" and also humanizing the working-class, working-poor, and poor people helps students take an objective look at damaging constructions of these groups. At the same time, discussions of middle-class issues show students from that socioeconomic level that their lives are not as secure as they might have believed; indeed, they might have more in common with people below them on the economic ladder than with those above.

Self-Assessment/i>clicker Questions

- Are you: A) Poor; B) Working Class; C) Lower Middle Class; D) Middle Class; E) Upper Middle Class; or F) Upper Class?

- If people worked harder, they would not be poor. Do you think this is: A) True or B) False?

- The United States is basically classless. A) Yes, B) No

- Rich people have worked very hard to get where they are. A) Yes, B) No

- Immigration hurts the economy. A) Yes, B) No

- Do you think social welfare programs A) help or B) hurt people?

- Do you think race makes class disparities worse? A) Yes, B) No

- Women are paid just as much money as men. A) Yes, B) No

Issues and Questions to Consider

- What is "middle class"? Are we a country of middle-class people? Or are we a classless society? What *is* class, then?

- Holly Sklar, in "Imagine a Country—2006," cites a number of problems that occur in the United States, and points out the contradiction that the richest country in the world has such troubles. Many students, though, become frustrated that Sklar names the problems but does not propose any solutions. They can be overwhelmed by the amount of information she provides. Discuss with them why this might be so. Does their experience with information sources provide them with detailed information about the world in which they live? What sorts of information do they have access to regarding economics in this country? Whose interests do the media represent? And, finally, why doesn't Sklar provide solutions to the numerous problems she names? Is that her job?

- How does race get factored into economics? Spend some time going over statistics in "Wealth Gap Between Races Widens" by Genaro C. Armas, in Dalton Conley's discussion of the wealth gap between white and minority families, and in the pieces of Meizhu Lui et al. on Latino/as and Asian Americans. Does everyone have an equal chance to make a lot of money in this country? Also look at the profiles Mantsios constructs in Part II. Why does one of the people described in the essay have so much more opportunity than the others in it?

- Discuss the work ethic and the American Dream. What do students think these are? Students will probably be struck by "Billionaires R Us" and "The Sons Also Rise," which should lead to some interesting discussions about the work ethic. This is especially true if you then look at Herbert's article on poverty or "The Education of Jessica Rivera." Are the people these authors discuss "lazy"? Do they lack an

ASSIGNMENT 10. After reading the articles in Part V—especially "US Poverty Rate was Up Again Last Year" (V, 2), "Wealth Gap Between Races Widens" (V, 3) and "The Wage Gap and its Costs" (V, 11)—turn to Part IX and read "Narrowing the Income Gap between Rich and Poor" (IX, 12), in which Michael Hout and Samuel R. Lucas argue that a solution to this problem (among others) is a revitalized labor union movement. Write a research paper in which you discuss what unions can and cannot do for working people. You might do some research on the history of the labor movement, a particular industry or strike, or a specific leader. As the authors have asked you to do throughout this text, however, avoid easy answers and stereotyping. Really dig in and investigate why Hout and Lucas make the claim that they do in their article.

ASSIGNMENT 11. After reading the two pieces by Meizhu Lui et al. (V, 8, 9) and Portes's piece (V, 16), write a research paper in which you analyze the impact recent waves of immigration have had on the economy. People like to say that illegal immigrants particularly "drain" the economy and "steal" jobs. Do they? What does immigration add to the economy? You might choose one group to focus on.

Recommended Media

- Be sure to show the PBS documentary on class, *People Like Us*. This video, which combines satire with hard statistics, is one of the best, most accessible discussions of class in America. It covers issues of race and ethnicity, gender, food, and social practices. It also does not avoid detailing the lives of the upper classes, thus giving students a full view of status—or lack thereof—in the United States today.

- Show a documentary that depicts either a historical or a contemporary labor issue, such as *Miles of Smiles, Years of Struggle: The Untold Story of the Black Pullman Porter*; *The Fight in the Fields: Cesar Chavez and the United Farm Workers*; *With Babies and Banners* (which is about women's role in the 1930s sit-down strikes at General Motors); *American Dream* (which is about a strike at a Hormel meat-packing plant); or *Harlan County, USA* (which is about a coal miners' strike in West Virginia in the 1970s). How do labor unions or collective labor consciousness help workers? You may have to spend some time breaking through students' misconceptions of unions. These films are a good way to get them thinking from the perspective of workers, rather than from that of owners/managers.

- Along these same lines, show John Sayles's fictional film *Matewan*, which tells the story of a miners' strike in a small town in West Virginia in the 1920s. The film deals with issues of both race and gender along with economics and is an engaging way to show students the multiple intersections, within a historical context, of these axes.

- Show either *Roger and Me* or *The Big One*, both by Michael Moore. You can also refer students to Moore's website. Moore's humorous and satirical portrayals of

---

American Dream? What prevents them from achieving their dreams? How is it that government assistance has been demonized when it goes to the poor but not when it goes to the rich? What is the effect of myths about people who "make it" because of "hard work" (like Andrew Carnegie or the characters in the stories of Horatio Alger) on discussions of poverty and people who live impoverished existences? How do they serve to socially construct attitudes and stereotypes of the poor and maintain economic hierarchies by preventing discussions of the redistribution of wealth?

- Have a discussion about work and gender. Bernstein's article on the gap between women's and men's wages details the ways women can be financially vulnerable even if they've worked most of their lives. Many students—women in particular—might want to argue that they can "make it" if they work hard enough, that they won't have to rely on their husband's salaries, and that they won't have economic barriers when they begin—or end—their careers. This is a tough position to counter because many women students have such high hopes for themselves. It's important, then, to keep focused on systemic and structural issues surrounding economics and work, rather than on individual stories of achievement.

- Krugman makes points about the economics of the Bush administration and the war on terror. You could ask your students how they view the class status of many members of the Bush administration (including Bush himself), its economic policies, and the economic future of the country. Do they think there is a connection? What is it? What purpose does Krugman's article serve in reminding people that an upper class exists, that entrance into it is largely through inheritance, and that the people who hold the highest political offices are often members of it?

Assignments

Generating Ideas/Small-Group Discussions

ASSIGNMENT 1. Read Holly Sklar's essay (V, 1) and, in a small group, brainstorm some solutions to three of the problems she names. When the class gets back together, discuss the problems your group identified, why you chose to focus on those particular problems, and the solutions your group came up with. How does thinking about solutions alter the way you read the Sklar text? Is it helpful? How does her use of research and statistics add to or detract from her overall point? Why are statistics important?

ASSIGNMENT 2. In your journal, consider the income gap—the disparities of wealth and income that exist between the classes in this country. The question here is: should there be such disparity in how people live their lives? What economic stability can people expect? Is it fair that there is such a gap between the rich and the poor—or even between the rich and the middle class? Consider this quote from the article "Billionaires R Us" (V, 4): "Income inequality is now near all-time highs, with over 50 percent of 2004 income going to the top fifth of households, and the biggest gains going to the top 5 percent and 1 percent of households. The average CEO now takes home a paycheck 431 times that of their average worker." Look over the last few articles in Part V on education and health, and think about the founding principles of the United States regarding the social contract. Is such wealth disparity healthy in a democracy such as ours? In the land of freedom and equality, what does it mean that such a gap exists?

ASSIGNMENT 3. Many of the articles in Part V ask that you examine economics in the United States from a structural perspective: there are stagnant home ownership rates among people of color in comparison to growth rates among whites; there is still a persistent gap in earning between whites and people of color despite class level; poor and professional women alike are limited in terms of work and economics because of their gender; and wealth and power have concentrated even more in the upper classes. Choose one of the articles in Part V and, with a partner, map out the ways race and/or gender intersect with economics and how those intersections affect peoples' lives. For instance, if you look at "Being Black, Living in the Red: Wealth Matters" (V, 7), how does Conley chart the differences between two families with similar income levels? After you and your partner have drawn the map, take a moment with your partner first to think about the implications of the system the two of you have outlined and then to consider solutions. What can be done to control for race and/or gender and to close the gap between the haves and the have-nots—in a structural and systemic manner? Try to avoid solutions that focus on the individual at the expense of the systemic.

ASSIGNMENT 4. As a homework assignment or a page in your journal, discuss your aspirations for your economic future. Where do you think your desires came from? What do you want for yourself? What is your work ethic? Is it enough in the face of current economic trends? This assignment is not meant to burst your bubble or critique your aspirations but to help you see how you fit in the larger economic landscape: to see yourself as part of a larger structure. Think about yourself both as an individual and as part of a greater whole. How might society structure itself differently to help more people realize their potential? Does your class, gender, race, ethnicity, or sexual orientation affect what you see for your economic future?

Writing Assignments

ASSIGNMENT 5. Draw on your brainstorming session about problems in Sklar's article (V, 1) in order to write an essay about two or three issues your group discussed. What are *your* solutions to Sklar's problems? What would your world look like? How might you "imagine" a better country? If you want to argue against some of Sklar's points, how do you interpret her identification of problems differently? What counterarguments might you offer?

ASSIGNMENT 6. Using at least two of the essays in Part V, write an American Dream. What is it? Who has access to it? Is it a positive, usefu it detrimental to people? You might draw on some of the statistics Leor Malveaux (V, 6), Meizhu Lui et al. (V, 8, 9), "The Wage Gap and its C cite and then look at a personal narrative such as Kim Phillips-Fein's pie Rivera (V 13). It is up to you, however, to decide which essays you will c

ASSIGNMENT 7. After reviewing Kim Phillips-Fein's "The Educatic Rivera" (V, 13), discuss your views of welfare and social services for th they necessary? Why or why not? Do societies have a responsibility towa izens to their citizens in need? Why or why not? Would you replace w something else? What do you think has happened in this country as a r state and federal welfare "reforms" of a few years ago? What is the gene tion of people on welfare? How do you think this view developed? How d fit into the larger capitalist structure of the United States?

Research/Analysis Projects

ASSIGNMENT 8. What sorts of stereotypes exist about poor women? Po How do poor people view themselves, and why? Draw on Bob Herbert's poverty (V, 5), Kim Phillips-Fein's piece about Jessica Rivera and her sti obtain an education (V, 13), and Alejandro Portes's article on immigrants children, who are United States citizens (V, 16). In your view, do poor peop proper "work ethic"? How does an impoverished existence make one more ble to things like abuse, domestic violence, and unsafe and crowded livin tions? Can it be that peoples' fears of the urban, fears of poverty, fears of the have ties to economic conditions? What do you think? Write an essay in wl discuss several of these issues. You might research some particular conn such as those between domestic violence and poverty. Or you might exa study of an area, such as Feldman's (V, 14) on educational inequality or Re poverty and health (V, 15), and discuss its social implications. What does i about the ways economics determines or constructs peoples' lives and their s possibility for the future or even their expectation of being healthy into their years? Or you can survey a week's worth of media—TV, magazines, or n pers—for representations of poor people. What sorts of stereotypes are perpet What is the reality behind such stereotyping?

ASSIGNMENT 9. Go out and do your own research on two or three of the lems Sklar details in her essay (V, 1). How have other countries in the world with these problems? Are their solutions different from the solutions pursued i United States? Spend some time comparing differing approaches and then ide which ones you think work best and why.

the plight of working people in this country translate well for students. And he consistently turns the tables on those in power rather than on the powerless.

- For an early comedic look at working peoples' lives, show Charlie Chaplin's *Modern Times*. You might discuss the treatment of working people and also how workers represent their own lives.

- You might also do a slide show of documentary photographers' work on the poor, such as that of Lewis Hine in the early part of the twentieth century and the photography of Farm Security Administration artists in the 1930s like Walker Evans and Dorothea Lange (known for her famous "Dust Bowl Madonna" photo). Discuss the social value of depicting poverty. You might tie this discussion to Mantsios's piece in Part VIII on "Media Magic." What can people learn from seeing "how the other half lives"? What drawbacks might there be to this kind of work?

- For a humorous but extremely informative video, show PBS's *Affluenza*, which discusses the consequences of rampant consumerism in America and its ties to class and wealth. What do students think about the filmmakers' conclusions and solutions?

Many Voices, Many Lives: Some Consequences of Race, Class, and Gender Inequality

The power of many of the personal accounts in Part VI stems not only from their expressions of the pain and conflict in others' lives but also from our general lack of familiarity with other peoples' point of view. Students tend to respond strongly to this part of the book: the authors' personal narratives concretize the more abstract concepts from other parts, often in gripping ways. Thus, Part VI can provide you with powerful tools for encouraging students to think through the experiences of inequity—both in terms of their own lives and in terms of being sensitive to the conflicts others must live through. The consequences of social hierarchies are neither abstract nor purely perceptual (that is, thinking differently about them won't make them go away). They are material, and the operations of hierarchies can be observed in all aspects of day-to-day living. Several of these selections emphasize the ways that everyday details reveal the structures governing our lives, if we look carefully enough. But the personal focus in this part often leads students to individualize the problems the text has tried to emphasize as being systemic, *social* dilemmas. This is not to say that individuals don't experience these issues—they do, obviously. However, in thinking through these issues only from an individual perspective (which is what many students do early on in their educational careers), students can miss the big picture. The assignments in Part VI, then, are designed to keep students focused on the social framework as they respond to the essays. Many of the assignments, in fact, ask them to literally read the essays here through a lens constructed by something from elsewhere in the book.

Self-Assessment/i>clicker Questions

- Are peoples' personal stories important to listen to with regard to race, ethnicity, class, gender, sexuality, etc.? A) Yes, B) No

- Do you remember having an experience when your race or ethnicity was an issue? A) Yes, B) No

- Have you ever felt out of place or unwelcome because of your gender? A) Yes, B) No

- Do you think activities like playing football or dieting a lot are harmful to men and women? A) Yes, B) No

- Are one's childhood experiences important for one's sense of self later on? A) Yes, B) No

- Can people truly change in their attitudes toward: A) race or ethnicity; B) gender roles; C) sexual orientation; D) disability; E) class?

- When you consider your identity, do you focus first on: A) race; B) ethnicity; C) gender; D) sexual orientation; E) class; F) ability; G) none of the above?

Issues and Questions to Consider

- Review the census figures in Part III and use them as a preface for your initial comments on Part VI. What does it mean that America is more diverse?

- Ask students to identify moments in the readings in which daily life reveals social hierarchies. How effective is this device in conveying the pervasive quality of race, class, gender, and sexual constructions (Brave Bird, Wu, Jimenez, Mirikitani, Sabo, Gomez, Shange, Cofer, for example)?

- Part VI, more than any other part, demonstrates the ways in which privilege functions as loss; privilege can permit and deny us all sorts of knowledge (Cofer illustrates this point beautifully when she discusses how stereotypes of Latinas prevent people of other ethnicities from knowing the incredible richness not only of her Puerto Rican roots but also of the whole range of cultures that compose the Latin American world). Ask students what their socially constructed point of view permits them to see and what it keeps them from seeing. In other words, how does their subjectivity as particularly raced, classed, gendered, and so on individuals enable or prevent them from seeing how other people experience their lives?

- Does self-understanding assist in self-transformation or not (Wood, Avicolli, Allen)?

- What do these selections suggest about the possibilities for changing the racist and sexist attitudes of others? What is the role of education as a solution for ending racism (Fayad, Wood, Wu, Terkel)? Sexism (Cofer, Avicolli, Gerhart, Chung, Griscom)? What is the significance of political action, and what conditions give rise to an individual's political involvement (Zirin, Kochiyama, Mayhew, Copeland, Terkel)?

- Class, gender, race and ethnicity do not map across each other in neat, predictable ways. Several selections underscore how complicated these intersections can be. For example, how does class position shift the significance of one's gender (Jordan, Coontz)? One's race or ethnicity (Mirikitani, Cofer, Kashef, Berger)?

- How does a person of mixed heritage expose the lie of racial categories? How does the notion of racial purity complicate racial identity (Fayad, Casares, Gomez, Chung)?

- The constructed nature of sexuality can be seen most readily when we resist the constructions and try to make visible the codes of masculinity, femininity, and heterosexuality. Students may benefit from reviewing Part I to address this issue (Cofer, Sabo, Avicolli, Copeland, Gerhart, Allen).

- Spend some time discussing masculinity and violence with your students. How do they define each other in many ways? (Sabo, Zirin, Beckman, Jordan) How do race and class intersect with violence and masculinity? (Jordan, Zirin)

- Because many of the essays in this section are stories, you might spend some time with the class discussing the role of narration in the construction of peoples' lives. How do the authors "write" themselves?

Assignments

Generating Ideas/Small-Group Discussions

ASSIGNMENT 1. Many of the essays in this section draw attention to the fact that they are stories, narratives of their authors' lives. How do we create our own lives through the stories we tell about ourselves? How can we "author" our lives? How can't we? And how do our stories of our past influence the way we live presently? Consider these questions in your journal, and bring your answers to class.

ASSIGNMENT 2. Go over "Civilize Them with a Stick" by Mary Brave Bird (VI, 1). You might think about the piece in Part IV that mentions an English-only policy in a restaurant next to the Navajo Reservation. Consider what it is and was to be a "Native" American in the United States. Why were Native-American children taken from their families and forced into boarding schools? What does Brave Bird mean when she talks about "white man's time as opposed to Indian time, which is natural time. Like eating when you are hungry and sleeping when you are tired, not when that damn clock says you must" (VI, 1)? Why do you think Rothenberg chooses to begin Part VI with this selection? Think about these questions for 10 minutes. Take notes on a sheet of paper; then meet with others in a small group to discuss your answers.

ASSIGNMENT 3. Read Sabo's "Pigskin, Patriarchy, and Pain" (VI, 13), Beckman's "How to Sell Humvees to Men" (VI, 15), Avicolli's "He Defies You Still" (VI, 16) and Thompson's "A New Vision of Masculinity" (IX, 3); review Lorber's "'Night to

His Day': The Social Construction of Gender" (I, 5), Kimmel's "Masculinity as Homophobia" (I, 8), and Johnson's "Patriarchy" (II, 6). What is masculinity? How do masculinity and patriarchy intersect? How does masculinity depend on homosexuality for its definition? How do stereotypes of homosexual behavior support the belief that homosexuality and masculinity are contradictory constructions? How does homosexuality seemingly (but not actually) interfere with the construction of masculinity? How do some of these authors experience their masculinity? Consider these questions in a 1–2 page journal entry.

ASSIGNMENT 4. With others in a small group, survey all of Part VI and decide which piece the group members all liked the best. Choose a note taker and discuss the article. What compelled you about it? What did the members of your group learn from it? How does it tie into previous parts of the text? How does it tie into previous essays in the text? The group should share its discussion with the rest of the class.

ASSIGNMENT 5. Read June Jordan's "Requiem for the Champ" (V, 18). In a journal entry, consider Jordan's use of words such as "winning" and "fighting." What have these words come to mean for her? What is she concerned with? What does "requiem" mean and why has Jordan written one? What perspective on economic success does she offer that the sports hero stories overlook? Be sure to take into account the analyses of masculinity, athleticism, and violence provided by Sabo (VI, 13) and Kimmel (I, 8).

ASSIGNMENT 6. Read the interview with C. P. Ellis conducted by Studs Terkel (VI, 28). Ellis comes to understand the role that racial hierarchies play in maintaining class hierarchies, and it is through this understanding that he begins to dismantle his racism. Seemingly minor episodes, such as walking down a street, were the basis for his self-understanding and transformation. Identify the moments when Ellis first begins to see the social structures that organize his life. What can one learn from Ellis's transformation? Consider these issues for about 15 minutes. Take notes on a sheet of paper; then meet in a small group to discuss your answers.

ASSIGNMENT 7. Part VI illustrates the many ways in which the ordinary episodes of daily life are affected by the social constructions of race, ethnicity, class, gender, sexuality, parenthood, and ability. It might seem as though these details are informed by personal choice, but consider instead how these so-called choices are affected by one's class and gender position. Working in a pair, consider the details of your daily lives: attempt to map the categories of race, ethnicity, class, sexuality, gender, and ability across them. For example, does class influence your selection of foods? Your clothing? Your hobbies and interests? The way you are able to raise your children? Does your race or ethnicity affect what school you attend and what careers are available to you? Does either or both influence how and where you spend your summers? Does your gender affect what you choose to study at college or which sports you participate in? When your class reconvenes, compare your pair's comments and observations with those of others.

Writing Assignments

ASSIGNMENT 8. For people going into "helping professions" such as teaching, social work, or counseling, listening openly and compassionately to other peoples' stories is important work. Really paying attention not only to how people narrate their lives but also to what individual experiences they have had will enable you to challenge your assumptions about those different from yourself. In an essay, choose one or more of the pieces from Part VI and discuss how you might use the insights the author conveys to you. What can you learn from listening to how someone tells her or his story? Later, how might this make you better able to help others? What assumptions did you discover you needed to challenge? How were they challenged?

ASSIGNMENT 9. Cofer describes what it is like to be treated as "a character" in a "cartoon-populated universe" (VI, 4). Several selections in Part VI (Wu, Cofer, Fayad, Casares, Gomez, Kashef, Chung, Gerhart) demonstrate the impossibility of escaping entirely the effects of media-generated race and gender stereotypes, regardless of one's class position or education level. In an essay, trace the effects of race and gender stereotypes through these selections and others in the book and in your own life. As an added dimension to your analysis, consider Snyder's (VIII, 1) and Miller's (I, 11) arguments for the self-fulfilling nature of stereotypes. What coping mechanisms do people devise? What conclusions can you draw about identity? How much of *who* we are is socially constructed?

ASSIGNMENT 10. Read Griscom's "The Case of Kowalski and Thompson: Ableism, Heterosexism, and Sexism" (VI, 26) and Davies's "Lame" (VI, 27). In both articles, the authors take care to articulate the interlocking strands of social resistance, the multiple modes of oppression that disabled women suffer. Write an essay in which you describe the three modes of oppression endured by Kowalski, Thompson, and Davies. Define ableism, heterosexism, and sexism, and describe how these combine to create additional obstacles in these women's lives. What do the non-disabled take for granted? What do you make of Davies's use of the term "lame" to describe herself? Why does she do this? How do the fears of disability mirror the fears and ignorance of homosexuality? Are the three oppressions similar, or do they differ? You may want to review Baynton's "Disability and the Justification of Inequality in American History" (I, 9), Frye's "Oppression" (II, 5) and Ettelbrick's "Confronting Obstacles to Lesbian and Gay Equality" (VII, 23).

Research/Analysis Projects

ASSIGNMENT 11. Consider Don Sabo's "Pigskin, Patriarchy, and Pain" (VI, 13), Ann Gerhart's "More and More Young Women Choose Surgical 'Perfection'" (VI, 22), and Alex Williams' "Before Spring Break, the Anorexic Challenge" (VI, 24), and write a paper in which you explore the costs of gender construction. You might collect ads or fashion layouts from magazines such as *Glamour, Mademoiselle, Seventeen, Elle*, and the like, and compare them to sports figures in *Sports Illustrated* or male models in *GQ, Details*, or *Maxim*. How are femininity and masculinity constructed through the media? What ideal is presented to people? How is that ideal achieved? What are the costs? At the end of your paper, discuss the implications of your findings for future generations. Are we headed down a "healthy" path? Why or why not?

ASSIGNMENT 12. Using Kochiyama's oral history "Then Came the War" (VI, 2), research Japanese internment in World War II and write a paper about it. Was this action justified? Why or why not? You might also look at Fayad's piece "The Arab Woman and I" (VI, 5) and think about it in the current context in the United States in the wake of the September 11, 2001 terrorist attacks in New York and Washington, D.C., the ensuing "War on Terror," the 2003 commencement of a war against Iraq, and the imprisonment of detainees in Guantanamo Bay. How close is the United States currently to replicating with Arab Americans or people of the Muslim faith its treament of Japanese Americans during World War II? Is the loss of civil liberties to this extent ever justified? Why or why not? What do the terms "freedom" and "liberty" mean? How does an event such as 9/11 strip away social conventions and allow people to act on their fears? You could look up the Patriot Act, which was passed by Congress right after September 11, 2001 and renewed recently, in order to provide even more context for answering some of these difficult questions.

ASSIGNMENT 13. Interview one or more family members to create your own oral history on the subject of race or class relations. Ask your subjects to relate as many details of their lives as possible to help you understand the period of time they are describing. How do they explain their beliefs and actions? Have those beliefs changed? How do they explain those changes? Were the changes the result of dramatic events, or did they come through a slow process of "unlearning"?

ASSIGNMENT 14. Your task in this assignment is to reflect about yourself in relation to others—in this case, other texts in *Race, Class, and Gender in the United States*. Write an essay in which you "narrate yourself." To do this, select a seemingly minor moment from your past (such as a conversation with a family member or an encounter with a stranger) that encapsulates within it some feature of your life whose significance you may not have understood at the time or may still need to figure out. You may use one episode or a series of small events. It can be a dream, a conversation, or a routine part of your day. The point is to select some moment or set of moments through which you've come to understand the significance of your place in the race, class, and gender hierarchies that organize your daily life. How are the material conditions of your life shaped by your place in the social scheme? Draw on selections from Part VI to help you clarify your experiences. "Narrating yourself" in this assignment means "you, in relation to your social and cultural context."

Recommended Media

- Show the film *Faces of the Enemy*, directed by Sam Keen, to illustrate the media's role in demonizing groups generally deemed "the enemy." (The video has a book that accompanies it.) You could also ask students to name who the "enemies" are in current thrillers. Are they "Americans"? Or are they "others"? What sorts of "others" do they tend to be?

- Show John Sayles's *Lone Star*. This film is useful for illustrating the intersections of family history and community history and what those intersections reveal about race and gender categories. Trace each story line. How does the film help students understand the way racial categories are maintained? What does the film say about borders? About racial mixing? What do students make of the ending? How can it be read as metaphorical?

- Show *Smoke Signals*, which depicts a kind of contemporary vision quest by its main character. Discuss what the film does with Native American stereotyping. What does the main character learn by the end of the film? You could also pair this film with clips from *Windtalkers*, a film starring Nicolas Cage that supposedly details the experiences of Navajos who were enlisted in the military during World War II to create a new code based on their language. Have students read the article in Part IV on Navajos being discriminated against for speaking their own language in the workplace and then discuss that in relation to these two films. What stereotypes does *Windtalkers* rely on to tell its story? How does *Smoke Signals* challenge those stereotypes?

- Show *Return to Paradise*, which is a Hollywood-ized love story between a Japanese American woman being held in an internment camp and a white soldier. You might also refer students to the Manzanar website for historical background on Japanese American internment. How much do students know about this period in American history? How successful have efforts been to recover this history?

- Show *Mississippi Masala*, and discuss how the film deals with interethnic issues.

- You could also show *Tortilla Soup* as a light-hearted look at a Mexican American family negotiating with the contemporary world. Have students look for the ways the film deals not just with ethnicity, but also gender—especially in the opening scenes in which the patriarch of the family makes a huge meal for his daughters. Other films that deal with Mexican American life in the United States include *My Family* and *Mi Vida Loca (My Crazy Life)*, which explores gang life from a girl's perspective.

- For a light-hearted look at the dysfunctionality of suburban families, you might show an episode of Comedy Central's cartoon series *South Park* and have students analyze what the makers of the series are spoofing.

How It Happened: Race and Gender Issues in U.S. Law

Part VII is an invaluable section in that it demonstrates to students how race, ethnicity, class, gender, and sexuality have been institutionalized and regulated throughout the history of the United States. Because this part is composed almost entirely of legal documents such as texts of laws, court decisions, and the like, it is one of the most flexible in the book. It particularly lends itself to research projects, as these documents appear without specific historical context. You may also choose to assign isolated selections to accompany other readings in the book (such as Kochiyama [VI, 2] with *Korematsu v. United States*). The absence of historical context can be a classroom virtue because you can ask students to think of these selections as constituting a "text" that critiques the notion of American justice as applied to women, persons of color, and nonheterosexuals. You can also have students go out and do their own research to provide the historical context for particular documents. Because this critique is found in the words of the documents themselves, students will discover irrefutable evidence for the history of oppression in this country. Remind students that these documents are not ancient history and that many of these courtroom battles are still being fought in various ways.

Self-Assessment/i>clicker Questions

- Were you aware that laws regulating interracial marriage existed? A) Yes, B) No
- When the United States was founded, every person was considered a citizen. This is: A) True or B) False
- How long have U.S. women had the right to vote in national elections? A) Since 1776; B) Since 1783; C) Since 1865; D) Since 1920; E) Since 1962
- Were slaves considered to be fully human? A) Yes, B) No
- Once the Civil War was over, there were no more laws regulating the rights and/or citizenship of African Americans. This is: A) True or B) False
- The Equal Rights Amendment was passed into law in the 1970s. This is: A) True or B) False

- Homosexual people have never had to contend with any laws aimed at controlling their behavior. This is: A) True or B) False

Issues and Questions to Consider

- What are the conditions for citizenship, as revealed in these documents (*Dred Scott v. Sandford*, "The Black Codes," the California Constitution, *People v. Hall*)? How does what these show compare with the essays in Part II?

- Trace the notion of justice as it appears in the documents in Part VII. Who is the Supreme Court actually protecting in cases such as *People v. Hall*, *Korematsu v. United States*, and *Elk v. Wilkins*?

- Many people believe that women have only fairly recently fought for their rights. However, the sheer number of court cases and legal rulings on the rights of women suggests that women have worked hard for legal and social equality for over a century and a half. Given the number of cases addressing the rights of women, does it appear that women have been content with their legally prescribed role? Whose interest does the narrative of "recent change" serve? What do the documents in this part suggest? (See "Declaration of Sentiments and Resolutions, 1848"; "The Antisuffragists: Selected Papers, 1852–1887"; *Minor v. Happersett*, 1874; *Bradwell v. Illinois*, 1873; United States Constitution: Nineteenth Amendment, 1920; *Roe v. Wade*, 1973; Equal Rights Amendment).

- How significant is the right to vote? Does it matter that the right to vote has been denied to over half the population for most of the U.S.'s history (Fifteenth and Nineteenth Amendments)?

- What should the constitution protect? What does "equal protection under the law" mean (Ettelbrick)?

- Ask students to review Holly Sklar's "Imagine a Country" in Part V in the context of the materials in Part VII. Did they know that the legal history of the United States shows how so many human and civil rights abuses were legally sanctioned, even enabled? Have the documents in Part VII caused them to think differently about the notion of justice?

- Given the historical inequities contained here, discuss some current legal issues, such as affirmative action or immigration reform, with students.

Assignments

Generating Ideas/Small-Group Discussions

ASSIGNMENT 1. After reading the "Declaration of Sentiments and Resolutions" (VII, 5), and "The Antisuffragists: Selected Papers, 1852–1887" (VII, 6), review

Frye's "Oppression" (II, 5). Working in a small group, discuss the Seneca Falls and the antisuffragist documents. List the reasons that women wanted full political participation, and list the variety of rationales offered for denying women the right to vote and participate as full citizens in the political body. What do you think about these rationales? Do they seem appropriate to their time period? Whose interest do they serve? In class discussion, compare your group's observations with those of other groups.

ASSIGNMENT 2. In the context of recent debates about gay marriage and domestic partnership legislation, read *Bower* v. *Hardwick* (VII, 22) and Ettelbrick's "Confronting Obstacles to Lesbian and Gay Equality" (VII, 23). Working in a small group, identify Ettelbrick's argument about civil rights protection for gays and lesbians. List each of the obstacles she identifies. In class discussion, try to come to consensus on the future of full legal equality for gays and lesbians. Is Ettelbrick optimistic or pessimistic? Use evidence from the essay to support your view.

ASSIGNMENT 3. Working in a pair, compare the language used to describe black Americans in *Dred Scott* v. *Sandford* (VII, 8) with the language the U.S. Commission on Human Rights identified as used to describe Native Americans in "Indian Tribes: A Continuing Quest for Survival" (VII, 1). Now look at the language used to describe women in *Bradwell* v. *Illinois* (VII, 12). What similarities can you identify in the attitudes held toward these groups of people? What effect did these attitudes have? How have these attitudes shaped history? In class discussion, compare your pair's observations with those of other pairs.

ASSIGNMENT 4. Read "The Black Codes" (VII, 11). W. E. B. Du Bois provides an account of the systematic attempts to deprive black Americans of their full and fair social and economic livelihood. In your journal, reflect on what the Black Codes mean for American history. Is this a different view of American history from what you have been taught thus far? What do the Black Codes reveal about whites?

Writing Assignments

ASSIGNMENT 5. The Seneca Falls Convention drafted the "Declaration of Sentiments and Resolutions" (VII, 5), deliberately modeled on the Declaration of Independence. Write an essay comparing the two documents. What was the strategic purpose of modeling the one document on the other? Was this effective, do you think? Why or why not?

ASSIGNMENT 6. Read *Korematsu* v. *United States*, 1944 (VII, 18), closely—especially the introductory section on the historical/political context of this document.

The Supreme Court defended the military's practice of wartime incarceration of Japanese Americans on the basis of national security, claiming that it was not an instance of racial discrimination and that "To cast this case into outlines of racial prejudice . . . merely confuses the issue." Assess the court's claim. Remember to keep in mind other readings in the collection, such as those of Omi and Winant (I, 1), Sethi (II, 4), and Kochiyama (VI, 2). You might also go look up the text of the Patriot Act and think about what that text codifies with regard to issues of national security and civil liberties.

ASSIGNMENT 7. Read *People* v. *Hall, Elk* v. *Wilkins* (VII, 15), and *Korematsu* v. *United States* (VII, 18). What notion of nationalism emerges from these cases? Write an essay on American nationalism in which you consider *who* is an "American." On the basis of court cases such as these, consider the differences between the real and the ideal notion of America. Rely on writers such as Brodkin (I, 4) and Kochiyama (VI, 2) to confirm or complicate your observations.

Research/Analysis Projects

ASSIGNMENT 8. *Brown* v. *Board of Education of Topeka*, 1954 (VII, 19) is a landmark case, but this court victory was long fought for and hardly the triumph of justice that we like to imagine. Few realize that *Brown* was built on many school desegregation cases before it. The *Brown* decision should be remembered in terms of the long education struggle—lasting more than 100 years—that preceded it, and the subsequent failure of governments to desegregate the schools even in the present. For this project, research the history of the school desegregation court cases and the *Brown* decision. You might start by referring back to Jeffrey Gettleman's article "The Segregated Classrooms of a Proudly Diverse School (IV, 19) for an overview. Was *Brown* universally endorsed by African Americans? Why or why not? How much time elapsed after *Brown* before school desegregation was enforced nationwide? What factors continue to present obstacles to equal educational facilities and opportunities? What does the history of the case and its context suggest about the role of the legal system in race relations?

ASSIGNMENT 9. Research the history of the Equal Rights Amendment. How long were women fighting for this amendment? What is its significance? Why was it defeated? List as many factors as you can find. Do you think it would have been a worthwhile addition to the Constitution? Why or why not?

ASSIGNMENT 10. Research the history of sexual harassment. When did sexual harassment become a crime? When was it widely recognized as a problem? When did suing employers for harassment become acceptable for women? Refer to "Women in the State Police, Trouble in the Ranks" by Jonathan Schuppe (IV, 6),

"Manhattan Store Owner Accused of Underpaying and Sexually Harassing Workers" by Steven Greenhouse (IV, 8) and "North Carolina State U. is Ordered to Pay $300,000 in Sexual Harassment Case" (IV, 9) to flesh out your discussion. You might also consider interviewing members of your family that have been in the workforce for at least 20 years. What do they remember about harassment in the workplace? Do they agree on what harassment is? Do they think that greater social recognition of the problem is a positive development?

ASSIGNMENT 11. After examining "The Antisuffragists: Selected Papers 1852–1887" (VII, 6), spend some time researching feminism and women's rights in the media. Listen to Rush Limbaugh or other AM talk radio personalities, watch some Fox News talk shows (especially *The O'Reilly Factor*), or just tune in to CNN, MSNBC shows, or the nightly news on TV and assess how women and women's rights are covered. What are the parallels to the antisuffragists' arguments? What are the implications of those parallels?

ASSIGNMENT 12. After reviewing "Indian Tribes: A Continuing Quest for Survival" (VII, 1), *Elk v. Wilkins* (VII, 15), and "Civilize Them with a Stick" by Mary Brave Bird (VI, 1), research some aspect of the history of Native American relations in the United States. You may choose to focus on more distant history — the Indian Wars, the establishment of the reservation system, boarding schools, etc., — or more recent events — the American Indian Movement (AIM), Indian gaming, the mascot controversies, and so on. Make sure to weave together the specific and the structural. Don't just make this a report; analyze your information as you go along. Why has the U.S.'s relationship with indigenous people been so complicated? Did it have to be that way? Why or why not?

ASSIGNMENT 13. Research the history of affirmative action. Why was it created? Is it still necessary? Consider the implications of the controversy over the University of Michigan's School of Law's admission policy of making race one of the categories that can help a student be admitted to the program. Given the history of race, race relations, and structural discrimination in the country, is this policy fair? Why or why not? Make sure you define your terms in your paper and provide specific examples.

Recommended Media

- Show the documentary *The Spirit of Crazy Horse* (PBS Videos), which is about the conflict between the Lakota people and the FBI on the Pine Ridge reservation. The film focuses on issues of citizenship, government mendacity and control, and a people's ability to determine their own lives and identity. What does this film illustrate about the lives of American Indians in this country? What does the film demonstrate about the definition of "American"?

- There are also several other video series on Native American tribes in the United States: *500 Nations*, *The Native Americans*, and *How the West Was Lost*. These can provide a great deal of context.

- You might consider showing all or part of the recent documentary series *Africans in America*, which is a fairly comprehensive history of slavery in the United States. Along these lines, the classic series *Eyes on the Prize* will give a pretty thorough view of the civil rights movement.

- *Daughters of the Dust*, directed by Julie Dash, tells the story of an extended African American family in the 1920s who leave their island community for the United States. The film allows you to discuss issues of history (the great migration, economic necessity, slavery, intraethnic relations) and other aspects of African American culture (such as dialect).

- Both *Chicano!* and *Viva la Causa: 500 Years of Chicano History* give overviews of Mexican Americans in U.S. history.

- In *Century of Women* (TBS documentary miniseries; six parts, 45 minutes each), several episodes provide historical context for the documents in Part VII. "Work and Family" and "Sexuality and Social Justice" trace policy decisions and other historical events affecting women from suffrage to civil rights to the Equal Rights Amendment and sexual harassment. Ask students to draw connections between the film and the documents they've read.

- Along these lines, *Not for Ourselves Alone: The Story of Elizabeth Cady Stanton and Susan B. Anthony* (PBS) is a documentary by Ken Burns on the early suffrage movement.

- You might also have students look up on the Internet the texts of fairly recent legislation, for example, California's antiimmigrant Proposition 187 (which was challenged in the courts) or Proposition 209, which effectively ended affirmative action on the state level in California. How do these propositions fit in with the rest of U.S. legal history?

Maintaining Race, Class, and Gender Hierarchies: Reproducing "Reality"

Overt social control, such as unfair laws or even state-sponsored violence, is easy to spot. Not so easy to identify are the myriad ways that "reality" is reproduced for U.S. citizens on a daily basis via the media, advertising, capitalism, the political system, the educational system, the prison system; indeed, by the very words we use and the images with which we surround ourselves. The challenge of Part VIII lies in conveying to students how reality is constructed through these various hierarchical structures—that power operates through the systems we've set up to organize our society. These systems work to not only create their and our own realities, but also to maintain hierarchies of privilege that pit people against each other and against themselves. Whether it's the ways heterosexuals set themselves up against gays, or how girls try to attain the "perfect" body, or how capitalism and desire are joined together by the advertising industry to turn our innermost desires against ourselves, these hierarchical systems dominate our lives and keep us from living in a more equitable society. Many students will resist efforts to unpack these systems, for such a project seems overwhelming or useless. However, showing students that mapping these systems actually gives *them* power to define their own realities can help them feel emboldened. Therefore, it might be helpful to set the stage for Part VIII by their reviewing some of the personal narratives in Part VI that deal with the negative effects of the systems of domination in our culture to enable them to understand this section of the text.

Self-Assessment/i>clicker Questions
- Do you think TV is just entertainment and therefore harmless? A) Yes, B) No
- Advertising is designed to just sell things to us, so it can't hurt us at all. A) Yes, B) No

- Is reality socially constructed? A) Yes, B) No
- Do you ever see class represented on TV? A) Yes, B) No
- Does it matter how prisoners are treated? A) Yes, B) No
- Language helps determine social realities. A) Yes, B) No
- The U.S. educational system is inherently unequal. This is: A) True or B) False

Issues and Questions to Consider

- Stereotypes are effective because they seem invisible; they constitute the seemingly natural. Evidence of the supposed accuracy of prejudiced beliefs is that these expectations are made manifest in the behavior of others. Snyder makes us aware of the power we have over others to reproduce the evidence we may seek to justify our own discriminatory behavior. Ask students to discuss the role played by negative expectations in eliciting certain behaviors in others.

- Discuss the power of political language. You might define the terms "hegemony" (a dominant ideology or set of controlling ideas and beliefs) and go over Parenti's ideas about "plutocracy" and analyze how the news media perpetuates particular ways of seeing race, ethnicity, gender, sexuality, class, and ability. Refer to Parenti for this discussion.

- What is the role of experience in maintaining or refuting false beliefs? Can experience *always* be trusted? (Mohr)

- How do institutions such as schools, businesses, prisons, advertising, and the media maintain class divisions? Race divisions? Gender divisions? How do students internalize these lessons? (Berger, Hesse-Biber, Jhally, Parenti, Kozol, Davis, Mantsios, Smith)

- What are the effects of making class invisible? Who benefits from social inequities? Who really benefits from blaming the victim? In whose interests do such strategies work? (Berger, Hesse-Biber, Parenti, Mantsios, Ryan) Ask students to review Mantsios's essay in Part II as well.

- How is whiteness rendered invisible in American culture? How is blackness used to highlight or offset whiteness? How are images of people of color used to foster fantasies of white supremacy in the media? (Berger, Smith)

- Cultural ideals, such as standards of beauty, seem to have no relationship to questions of social power, but how do the rewards for thinness interfere with other kinds of social rewards women might aspire to? What does this connection suggest about the relationship between gender ideals and social and economic power? (Hesse-Biber) Ask students to also refer back to Gerhart's essay in Part VI.

- How does advertising lead to unhappiness? Discuss Jhally's points about consumer culture, the consumer ethos, and the happiness studies. Do your students like to shop? Do the things they buy make them happy? What are they buying when they respond to advertising campaigns?

- Are institutions in the United States designed by and for the rich, as Parenti claims? Have students think through his assertions and really consider the legal, educational, governmental, and media systems in which they operate.

- Violence and the threat of violence reinforce ideologies of difference by threatening those who might challenge the status quo. Ask students to name other forms of violence, such as sexual harassment, that function to keep people "in their place." (Mohr, Hesse-Biber, Chafe, Smith)

- Ask students to consider the usefulness of art—fiction, poetry, painting, performance, music, and so on—in identifying and describing social problems. Refer to the ways Chafe uses novels to illustrate his points. What is the role of art? Especially consider this question in light of how much image making is in the service of creating and maintaining social hierarchies in the popular culture. (Berger, Hesse-Biber, Mantsios, Jhally)

- Ask students to review Snyder's analysis of the psychology of bias in conjunction with Hesse-Biber's discussion of feminine beauty. How does self-hatred become internalized? How does internalizing such ideals reinforce them? What are the risks to women who refuse to conform to feminine ideals? What strategies can women adopt to work against these images?

- How do your students' experiences of school match up with those that Kozol outlines in his text? Ask students to interrogate their current educational environment in light of Kozol's discussion.

- How does Angela Davis make visible the structural inequalities inherent in the prison system in the United States? What points does she make? How do students respond to those points? Should we worry about how this country treats its prisoners? Why or why not?

Assignments

Generating Ideas/Small-Group Discussions

ASSIGNMENT 1. Spend a week doing an "ideology hunt" in the mass media. You may choose whatever sources you want: newspapers, magazines, TV shows, films, and so on. Collect clippings or write brief summaries of your observations, and then at the end of the week, in your journal, assess what you came up with. How many stereotypes did you encounter? How many times was whiteness depicted as the "norm"? How often was class erased or a middle-class point of view taken for granted? And so on. You might want to limit your search to just *one* particular ideological perspective to make this assignment more manageable. Share your discoveries with the class when you're finished.

ASSIGNMENT 2. Ryan argues that "blaming the victim" (VIII, 12) is a "warfare" strategy that begins with good intentions. The appeal of this ideology for the middle class is that it protects class interests while providing a rationale compatible with their morality. Thus, in Ryan's analysis, even well-intentioned people are part of the problem. In a 2-page homework assignment, discuss his analysis. How does sympathy, in certain forms, contribute to maintaining social inequities? For help in answering this question, you might refer to "Hospital Apologizes for keeping Black Workers from Patient's Room" (IV, 17) in which hospital administrators caved in to the demands of a racist husband of a patient that no African American doctors, nurses, or service employees be allowed in his wife's room. Can you think of additional examples of solutions that fall under Ryan's critique? Which solutions to social problems would Ryan approve of? Which ones does he reject and why?

ASSIGNMENT 4. Snyder argues that stereotyping "others" is deeply rooted and resistant to change even in the face of challenging evidence. In fact, he asserts, "Apparently good will and education are not sufficient to subvert the power of stereotypes" (VIII, 1). In your journal, write down examples of gender, race, sexuality, or class bias you suspect you engage in unconsciously. Analyze your own reaction times in situations where you deal with someone who is different from you or someone who you think is attractive or unattractive. Does being conscious of your own thought processes help or impair your ability to challenge bias in your mind?

ASSIGNMENT 5. Several of the essays in Part VIII proceed from the identification and analysis of cultural narratives, which are the stories or rationales people tell themselves to suggest that the social order is inevitable or, at least, that it makes sense. Examples are: "Boys are more rational than girls"; "Women need a man to take care of them"; "There will always be poor people because it's their fault they're poor, anyway"; "Blacks are lazy"; "Chicanos are have too many children "; "Asians are meek and hard workers"; "The Irish are heavy drinkers"; "Gays are mentally ill"; "Disabled people are incapable of doing complex tasks"; etc. Keep a journal entry for 1 week in which you write down every cultural narrative you hear someone use to rationalize a social condition or someone's behavior. Be sure to note the circumstance in which you heard it, and jot down any that you're uncertain of. At the end of the week, as a class, compile everyone's findings. What kinds of circumstances were explained by prejudiced or mistaken beliefs? How frequently were such rationales invoked? What do the narratives you heard say about your social environments?

Writing Assignments

ASSIGNMENT 6. Snyder discusses his research in which people act out or act on their stereotypes about who people are and what they're capable of (VIII, 1). Mohr describes the failure of empirical studies to dislodge stereotypes that have a "social function" (VII, 2). Both Snyder and Mohr suggest the limits of education and research to change people's minds about deeply rooted views. Yet, clearly, as Mohr puts it, a "willful ignorance of society's workings" greatly contributes to the perpetuation of false beliefs. These two writers believe in the importance of continued research and education to effect change. Write an essay in which you consider the value of education as a transformative enterprise.

ASSIGNMENT 7. Compare the theories of Miller (I, 11) and Chafe (VIII, 9) on how sexism and racism are maintained in U.S. society. Start by identifying the arguments each writer makes. Chafe claims that the analogy of sex and race is a useful explanatory model for oppression because, despite their differences, both women and persons of color endure the condition that "others have controlled the power to define one's existence." Similarly, Miller discusses our tendency to internalize beliefs and behaviors that mirror social expectations of us, even when such behavior is not in our best interest. Compare in detail the arguments made by each writer. Where do the writers differ in emphasis? Are their views compatible? How useful are these theories in explaining the ways that social hierarchies are maintained?

ASSIGNMENT 8. After reading Mantsios's "Media Magic" (VIII, 7), write an essay in which you discuss what else you think the media renders invisible other than, or in addition to, class. You could refer to Maurice Berger's piece "White Lies" (VIII, 3) if you want to bring in a discussion of how whiteness, unless we look at it carefully, is also made invisible in the media. Or you could use Sut Jhally's article "Advertising and the End of the World" (VIII, 5) to analyze the ways even our most intimate thoughts and feelings are exploited in order to sell us things. Choose some aspect of your life and discuss how the media frames it. What is made visible? What are you not encouraged to see? What is the effect of all this?

ASSIGNMENT 9. Read both Michael Parenti's "Plutocratic Culture" (VIII, 6) and Jonathan Kozol's "Still Separate, Still Unequal: American Apartheid Education" (VIII, 8) and discuss the ways Parenti's thesis might explain Kozol's findings. Who is able to "buy" the best schooling for their children? Why is such inequality, in a staunchly democratic nation, allowed to continue? In your essay, consider these questions and draw on your own educational experience if you'd like.

Research/Analysis Projects

ASSIGNMENT 10. Read Ryan's "Blaming the Victim" (VIII, 12), and pay particular attention to his example of lead paint posters. Find an example of a public service announcement currently being broadcast on your local or regional news. Research the issue the poster or ad addresses. Analyze the ad to determine who is being blamed. Who does the ad address? What type of solution does the ad advocate? Does your example bear out Ryan's argument?

ASSIGNMENT 11. In his article, Ryan discusses a little of the history of Social Darwinism. What is this? What is its history? Write a paper in which you first describe the history of this particular ideology and then discuss whether or not you think it's a thing of the past. Go back and survey some of the documents in Part VII from the nineteenth century and see if this ideology is manifested there. If you don't think Social Darwinism is a thing of the past, how is it currently manifested? Specifically, what beliefs or messages in American culture today manifest a Social Darwinist ideology? Look back over Parenti's piece "Plutocratic Culture" (VIII, 6). Do some of his ideas echo this ideology? A place to start on this project might be to survey current business practices and beliefs. What is the mantra for the proper way to run a business or corporation? What do business journals or magazines say about competition? Or you might consider the whole slew of reality shows on TV.

ASSIGNMENT 12. Andrea Smith's article "Sexual Violence as a Tool of Genocide" (VIII, 10) illustrates the role of violence in defining masculinity and exerting control over women, especially women of color. Select three different masculine icons from popular culture (e.g., one of the actors who played James Bond, or Sylvestor Stallone, Nicolas Cage, Arnold Schwarzenegger, Jean-Claude van Damme, Keanu Reeves, Tom Cruise, Ben Affleck, Wesley Snipes, Bruce Willis, Harrison Ford, Will Smith, Jackie Chan, etc.). Compare the masculine ideal that each of them portrays. Is violence a crucial dimension of their masculine identity? What kind of violent acts do they engage in? What other attributes can you identify by which we know they are *men*? Who do they dominate? On whose feminine bodies is their masculinity proven? Kimmel's "Masculinity as Homophobia" (I, 8) will also be helpful here.

ASSIGNMENT 13. Read Hesse-Biber (VIII, 4) and review Lorber (I, 5), Hubbard (I, 6), and Gerhart (VI, 22). Also look back over the essays discussing masculinity and men. Then, either watch commercials that are shown during a "woman's show" (soap operas, *Oprah Winfrey*, a women's sporting event, etc.) and a "man's show" (sports, news, an action show, etc.) or compile a selection of ads from women's and men's magazines for similar product lines. Compare the ways marketers target women and men. What did you find? How do advertisers construct gender differently in the commercials or ads? What assumptions do the ads seem to make about male and female consumers? How do those assumptions influence the ways women and men act? Feel? Think of themselves? Why do you think capitalism promotes gender differences in advertising? How does capitalism directly benefit from gender differences? You might refer to Sut Jhally's discussion of advertising's effects on our innermost desires to flesh out your analysis (VIII, 5).

ASSIGNMENT 14. Research and then write an essay in which you discuss the ownership and control of the media, with a specific focus on race and/or gender issues. Review Berger's (VIII, 3) and Johnson's (II, 6) articles in which they discuss the impact stereotypes promulgated by the mass media, controlled largely by white males, have had on women and people of color. What are the implications of our mass media being operated based on a narrow definition of what constitutes "normal"? *Who* is "normal" in the mediated world? And who isn't? Who gets stereotyped? And who doesn't? Why is this issue important to examine and understand? You might also consider Snyder's discussions of "self-fulfilling stereotypes" and the possible origin(s) of the negative feelings many whites have toward people of color (VIII, 1). Could media representations influence at a basic level how people view each other?

ASSIGNMENT 15. Read Mantsios's "Media Magic: Making Class Invisible" (VIII, 7). Tape or just watch and take notes of the local evening TV news on one station for a week. Either make an edited tape of news stories or summarize the stories you saw that illustrate Mantsios's points about the construction of class divisions. Study the stories in terms of the class narratives they offer. How are white-collar professionals depicted? How are the rural poor depicted? The urban poor? Can you identify patterns in the ways certain groups are depicted in your town or region? Are Mantsios's observations applicable? How? Did you see different narratives? What were they? Write an essay on your findings, and do a presentation on it in class.

ASSIGNMENT 16. Following Kozol's lead, visit some schools in your area (VIII, 8). Make sure you have a mix of low-income and upper-income areas that you target. See if you can observe some classrooms, interview students, teachers, and administrators, and record your findings. Write a paper in which you analyze your findings. What kind of curriculum was taught in poorer schools? What sorts of equipment did you see? How did the students relate to their schools? What were the teachers' experiences in the classroom with their students? Finally, what are your conclusions from your project? Do Kozol's observations apply to schools in your area? Why or why not?

ASSIGNMENT 17. After reading Davis's "Masked Racism: Reflections on the Prison Industrial Complex" (VIII, 11), research the history of the prison system in the United States and how it compares to other industrialized nations around the world. What does Davis mean by "masked racism"? How does she define the "prison industrial complex" in her essay? Why are so many people incarcerated in the United States today? How does that compare to incarceration rates in the past? What is the difference between an ideology of reform and an ideology of punishment? What do you think works best? Why? Write a paper that fully explores these questions in the context of the history of incarceration in the United States. Make sure you connect your discussion up with other concepts covered in the book so far.

Recommended Media

- Science-fiction films can offer a great deal of insight into the ways society organizes itself. Thus, for a simple, useful, and fun—albeit a bit crude—portrayal of how ideology works, show John Carpenter's cult classic *They Live*. Ask students to focus on the moment when the main character finally "sees" the ideological underpinnings of what he has previously taken for granted. Also ask students to think about what the aliens represent in the film. For a more current take on this issue, you might also show *Matrix* and its sequels.

- You might also directly address the power of blockbuster films to help create and maintain hierarchies. Compare and contrast how race and gender are dealt with in *Independence Day*, in which the white, male, middle-aged President of the United States is the one who accomplishes the final elimination of the alien invaders (Will Smith's fighter pilot notwithstanding), and a film like *Anaconda*, where one white male is disabled for almost the entire film and another is eventually eaten by a giant snake, leaving a young Latina (Jennifer Lopez) and a young African American man (Ice Cube) to save the day. These are perfect films to analyze in this context because they are not "arty" or "political" but, rather, as students always love to point out, "just entertainment." Have your students, then, discuss recent films that they've seen in this context.

- Show a "women's film" such as *Maid in New York* or *How to Win a Guy in Ten Days*. Ask students to analyze the film for its construction of femininity, masculinity, heterosexuality, gender relations, class, and race. What stories do these films tell women? What are the consequences of those stories? But also, why are they powerful? What hopes do they give women in particular?

- *Slim Hopes* or *Killing Us Softly III*, both directed by Jeanne Kilbourne, trace the media's use of women's bodies to sell products and examine the ways in which women's bodies simultaneously become objectified, commodified, and infantilized. In *Slim Hopes*, Kilbourne also addresses the causal relationship, if any, between eating disorders and such depictions. You might also consider showing Walt Disney's *Cinderella* in order to look at how even as children, girls are socialized to be pretty, masochistic, and competitive. If girls are meant to aspire to be Cinderellas, where does that leave them?

- Spike Lee's *Bamboozled*, paired with the documentary, *Ethnic Notions*, interrogate the long-standing, stereotypical depictions of African Americans in popular culture. Lee's film, a biting satire of the film and television industry, takes as its premise the creation of a *nouveau* minstrel show by an ambitious African American comedy writer. Pairing this often painful, often funny film with *Ethnic Notions*, which is referenced in *Bamboozled*, is a great way to introduce students to the long legacy of racist imagery in popular culture.

- Along these lines, you could also show *Color Adjustment*, directed by Marlon Riggs, which traces the history of the representation of black Americans on network TV in the United States and insistently poses the questions: What counts as a *positive* social image, and what counts as *negative*? Ask students to consider changes in the representation of black Americans since Riggs's film was made. You might also show a clip from *Birth of a Nation* to establish some of the historical context of media and societal representations of African American people.

- You might check out the Web site for the Media Education Foundation (www.mef.org). This nonprofit organization produces videos such as Sut Jhally's *Advertising and the End of the World*, which pairs well with his article in this section, details the pervasive ideological aspects of the advertising industry and their implication in major environmental disasters and *The Myth of the Liberal Media*, which offers a very useful outline and explication of Noam Chomsky's propaganda model of the media. Jean Kilbourne's videos are offered here, as are videotaped interviews with bell hooks, Edward Said, and Stuart Hall.

- You might also show students *The Corporation*, a documentary that very explicitly details how corporations operate. This would pair well with Parenti's piece in this section.

Social Change: Revisioning the Future and Making a Difference

By the time you come to the end of *Race, Class and Gender in the United States*, seventh edition, students might feel somewhat disheartened at the state of things in this country. Although many of the essays throughout the text offer solutions to the problems they name, students often come away with the sense that the articles have been primarily concerned with describing the inequities many Americans face. Part IX is designed to address such feelings by giving readers concrete strategies for enacting social change. The essays here enable them to re-envision the future, to "make a difference" in the world, and to offer alternative narratives for how our society can (and should) be. You may want to ask students to consider the generic distinctions between these selections and those in other parts. The assignments in this part are designed to focus students' attention on the details of the arguments presented here to help them acquire a critical vocabulary to use beyond the classroom. They are also designed to get students to think of or even create their own strategies to enact social change. Then, if inspired, students will be able to begin their own activist projects or, at least, to continue the difficult task of constructing their own critical lens through which to view the world in which they live.

Self-Assessment/i>clicker Questions

- An individual can enact social change. A) Yes, B) No
- Do you think collective action is a viable way to try to change things? A) Yes, B) No
- Can white people have a role in social movements regarding race? A) Yes, B) No
- Do you think feminism is: A) A good thing; B) A neutral thing; C) A bad thing
- Should men rethink masculinity? A) Yes, B) No
- Can people truly change? A) Yes, B) No

- Have you ever participated in a protest? A) Yes, B) No
- Would you consider yourself to be an activist? A) Yes, B) No

Issues and Questions to Consider

- Ask students what the value is of trying to change oppressive social systems. You might spend some time defining the term "utopia" (a good, basic definition is "the no place which is the good place," drawing on the Greek origin of the word) and tying it to the work of the authors in this part. Is "utopian thinking" hopelessly passé and ridiculously naive? Or is it a necessary impulse that sparks social change? Utopias have traditionally functioned as critiques of the author's own society. You might point that out to students as well.

- What does it mean to "redefine difference"? Ask students to consider why none of the positions set forth in Part IX suggest disregarding differences. You might refer back to the question concerning "color blindness" and "gender neutrality" in the "Issues and Questions to Consider" section of Part III in this manual. In whose interest is it to overlook differences?

- Blanchard takes issue with the school of thought that focuses on economic disparities as being more oppressive than racism. What do students make of his argument? What must "white folks" do to end racism?

- How does the "ally" model "interrupt the cycle of oppression"? Ask students to assess Ayvazian's use of this term and its effectiveness.

- Do the writers in this part argue for social change or social transformation? What's the difference between the two concepts? Which writers argue for "social change"? What are the conditions other writers identify as requiring transformation? What are the conditions they suggest that would make transformation possible? How have people engaged in transformative projects? You might spend some time with your students assessing the goals of the various activist projects Part IX includes.

- Attentiveness to the structure and detail of everyday life has been a constant thread throughout this volume, urging us to focus on the tangible and immediate rather than the abstract and transcendent. How does the discussion about the word "fag" that Cooper Thompson uses to begin his piece bring home the ways masculinity defines itself against women and homosexual men? Or Bronski describing holding his lover's hand on a public street? Or how do the articles about student activists force your students to think about the t-shirts they might be wearing? How do other authors use the category of the everyday and to what effect?

- These articles emphasize the necessity for the redistribution of power if any kind of meaningful social change is to be effected. Some students will find this liberating, but many will find it threatening, even those who might stand to gain the most from such change. Ask students to focus their attention on why these solutions are the ones selected to be in the volume. What does the magnitude of the proposed solutions suggest about the severity of the problems described? (Lorde, hooks, Ayvazian, Thompson, Blanchard, Hout, and Lucas)

- Ask students to consider how their lives would be different if fundamental social change were to occur. Would their lives improve or decline? What is their investment in maintaining things just as they are?

- Ask students if they have ever cared deeply enough about an issue to do something tangible about it. Are they members of any sort of activist groups? Why or why not? This would be a good place to discuss Pitts's entreaty to "Do Something." If students have "done something," is Pitts's plea enough? Do people need to do more to effect social change?

Assignments

Generating Ideas/Small-Group Discussions

ASSIGNMENT 1. Your instructor will bring a selection of colored pens, colored pencils, and some poster boards or large pieces of paper to class. Join a group of about four to five people. The group's task will be to draw a map of a utopia. Many people believe that a utopia is an ideal world. Others try literally to make a blueprint of a utopia—with varying results. An interesting pace to start from for this assignment is the notion that a utopia is "the no place which is the good place." In other words, it's a place that does not literally exist except in the ideal; it's an impulse, something to work *toward*. For this assignment, then, the group members can draw a literal map or draw a representation of their utopia. They should spend time negotiating what they want their utopia to be (which may be difficult since people may want different things). Make sure your group considers: race, class, gender, sexuality systems; economics; education; the environment; government; resources; and the like. How will the group's utopia deal with all of these? How will this new world be different from the one we live in now? When the map is finished, group members should spend some time summarizing their utopia to present it to the rest of the class. After every group has presented its utopia, review the definition stated previously: How does conceptualizing a different world help you think about the one we live in now? How does that impulse to conceive of "the good place" make you try to do something concrete? Does it make you want to do something here? Or is the gap between the actual and the ideal seem too large for you? On the other hand, how can a project like this open up your mind to think about things in new and different ways? Is there value in that?

ASSIGNMENT 2. In groups, identify a social issue that you want to do something about. You might review Sklar's essay "Imagine a Country—2006" (V, 1) for ideas to help you with this assignment. Be specific and focused. Map out a strategy for doing something about your issue. Use the articles about Students Against Sweatshops, volunteerism, or "take back the highway" as guides. When you're finished, re-convene with the rest of the class and present your plan.

ASSIGNMENT 3. Read the essays by Bronski (IX, 7) and "Rice Shirts Make More Than Fashion Statement" (IX, 8). Both pieces focus on the prevalence of homophobia in our society and how such attitudes threaten freedom of gays to function comfortably in U.S. society. Spend some time in your journal outlining each author's solution to combating homophobia. How do the pieces complement each other?

ASSIGNMENT 4. In a small group, review bell hooks's essay, "Feminism: A Transformational Politic" (IX, 2). Pay particular attention to the section where hooks outlines her vision of small group, or "kitchen table" discussion sessions. Choose someone to take notes and then discuss hooks's idea. Do you think a small group is a good "arena for education for critical consciousness"? How do you view small group work? Is it easier for people to talk to each other in such a setting? Present your discussion to the rest of the class and see what other groups came up with.

Writing Assignments

ASSIGNMENT 5. What student movements are happening on your campus? What do you think of them? Are you participating in any of them? How? Do you plan on joining one or more? Why or why not? Write a short essay in which you consider these questions. What does activism mean to you? What do you think it can do? Be sure to include specific examples with some assessment of these groups' efficacy, in your opinion. You might look over Gavin Leonard's piece "Rethinking Volunteerism in America" (IX, 5) and bring in a discussion of the difference between volunteerism and charity. Why do people get involved in various activist projects?

ASSIGNMENT 6. Read "Interrupting the Cycle of Oppression: The Role of Allies as Agents of Change" by Andrea Ayvazian (IX, 4). What is an "ally"? Does Ayvazian's use of the term provide an adequate model for people in dominant positions in the culture or people with relative power to enact social change? How? Write an essay in which you discuss Ayvazian's article and the term "ally." Make sure you provide some concrete examples in your paper.

ASSIGNMENT 7. According to Fletcher Blanchard (IX, 6), what must whites do to help end racism and bigotry? Write an essay in which you consider Blanchard's analysis of overt racism and unintentional, well-meaning bigotry. What do you think of this essay? What did you learn from it? In your estimation, will the author's solutions work? Why or why not?

ASSIGNMENT 8. In her essay, "Age, Race, Class, and Sex: Women Redefining Difference" (IX, 1), Audre Lorde unpacks the notion of "difference," outlining the ways we use differences to tear ourselves apart. Her solution is that rather than viewing differences negatively, we must celebrate difference, and use it as a way to bring ourselves together. bell hooks, in her essay, "Feminism: A Transformational Politic" (IX, 2), asserts that we must reclaim the notion of "love," in the broadest sense of the word. How do Lorde and hooks cover similar ground? What do celebrating difference and "loving" have to do with one another? Write an essay in which you explore these solutions. They are seemingly simple, yet hold a profound vision of a transformed society, so think hard on these ideas in your paper.

ASSIGNMENT 9. Select any one essay or article from Part IX. Write a summary of the argument and an explanation of the views presented. Be sure to pay careful attention to the specific positions the author holds. Use as much detail as possible to delineate the pains, challenges, and responsibilities emphasized in the essay. Focus on making the author's views clear to someone who has never read the essay.

Research/Analysis Projects

ASSIGNMENT 10. "Difference" is the basis for "identity politics," which emerged as a response to—and a rejection of—the integrationist politics of the 1960s, exemplified by the civil rights movement. Research the short history of identity politics. Why did it emerge? What are the arguments in favor of assimilation politics? What are the arguments for rejecting assimilation politics? Lorde (IX, 1), Blanchard (IX, 6) or Ayvazian (IX, 4) might help you get started.

ASSIGNMENT 11. Both Audre Lorde (IX, 1) and bell hooks (IX, 2) cite the work of Paolo Freire as instrumental in understanding how to teach a transformational politics. Do a research paper on this highly influential educator. You might read Freire's book, *Pedagogy of the Oppressed*, and think about his project. Review Jonathan Kozol's piece in Part VIII. How does one teach about oppression? How does one teach *to* the oppressed?

ASSIGNMENT 12. In her article, Ayvazian (IX, 4) mentions an exercise she does with groups she is speaking to in which she asks people to name some famous racists (which always gets a big response) and then to name some famous *anti*racists (which is largely met with silence). Taking Ayvazian's lead, write a research paper in which you discuss antiracism as a political practice and cite some people who have done work in this area. Some areas to look up: the abolition movement, the civil rights movement, the Black Power movement, the United Farm Workers struggles, the Chicano rights movement, the American Indian Movement, and so on. What can you learn from doing this research? What has been the role of allies in social movements? You could also do this paper from a gender, sexuality, or class perspective as well.

ASSIGNMENT 13. In "Combating Intentional Bigotry and Inadvertently Racist Acts," Fletcher Blanchard (IX, 6) describes an experiment he and his colleagues conducted in 1991, in which they briefly interviewed students about racism as the students walked between classes. The researchers would plant someone also walking by who would give programmed responses either expressing antiracist views or condoning racism. The subject of the experiment would then often follow suit. This finding led Blanchard to the conclusion that people need to take strong public stands against racism and bigotry to help end them. Working with others in a group project, look up Blanchard's original article in *Psychological Science* and reenact the experiment he and his colleagues conducted at your school. Write up the group's findings in a collaborative paper. Did your results mirror those of Blanchard and his colleagues? Or not? In what ways were your results the same or different? What did the members of your group conclude about Blanchard's solution to help end racism? Would it work? How?

ASSIGNMENT 14. In "Narrowing the Income Gap between Rich and Poor," Michael Hout and Samuel Lucas (IX, 12) argue that wealth needs to be re-distributed so that the huge gap between the rich and the poor is eliminated. To do this, they believe that a re-invigorated labor movement is key. In other words, unions "help lower the inequality of income because they typically make management more accountable to workers." After reading Hout and Lucas's article carefully, research some aspect of the history of the labor movement in the United States and write a paper about it. Pay particular attention to what the ability to unionize has done for workers. Why have people fought to the point of dying for the right to organize? Try to challenge your own assumptions about labor activism and unions in this paper. In whose interest has it been to paint labor activism as extremist and dangerous? Dangerous to whom? What are the implications of a unionized labor force? Refer back to Hout and Lucas to help you with your conclusion.

ASSIGNMENT 15. Read "Students Confront Sweatshops" by Richard Applebaum and Peter Drier (IX, 11). Research the history of Students Against Sweatshops and write an essay about contemporary student movements. Make sure to take into account students' increasing interest in issues of globalization and international politics. Is there a chapter of SAS on your campus? Should students consider their place in the move towards globalization? What *is* globalization?

ASSIGNMENT 16. Many students may feel challenged by the material in this text. This assignment is designed to give you a constructive way to channel your energies into a service-learning project. For this project, pick an organization, group, nonprofit agency, or the like, and volunteer your time (for ideas, think about the activist projects Woodard [IX, 9] and Hearn [IX, 10] write about in this section). Choose something that you feel passionate about and that has come out of the work you have done in this class. You might volunteer at a battered women's shelter or at a labor union. You could sign up to be a mentor or to teach an adult to read. Participate in a Meals-on-Wheels program. Whatever you decide to do, take notes on your experience. At the end of the class, write a paper in which you establish what your goals were as influenced by the readings in the book, what you accomplished in your position, and what you wish to do in this vein in the future. Make sure to review the steps Leonard (IX, 5) outlines in his essay on volunteerism to help guide you in your participation in the project you choose to focus on. In the face of the large-scale problems we have been studying, this may seem like a small step. However, as William Rivers Pitts reveals in "Here Now Do Something" (IX, 13), change occurs in the everyday, small actions one person does as well as on the large-scale level.

ASSIGNMENT 17. Review newspaper articles and other materials on the antiwar movement, both domestic and international, which grew up in response to the 2003 war in Iraq. How was this movement organized? What was significant about it? What happened to it? How did the mass media frame it? Use this movement as a recent case study for how social movements form, how they work, and what they do to enact social change. Make sure your essay introduces the context for the movement, as well as describes and analyzes the movement itself.

ASSIGNMENT 18. Do a research project on a social movement in the past. You might look over the documents in Part VII and think about the movements that helped usher in legislative reforms or the movements that formed in reaction to what some would see as legislative setbacks. You could also read through Howard Zinn's *A Peoples' History of the United States* to find a movement that appeals to you. Some questions you should ask yourself as you write this paper: What was the movement meant to accomplish? Was it successful? Why or why not? Make sure you cite specific examples and that you detail what the movement achieved.

Recommended Media

- If you want to do a unit on utopia/dystopia, you might begin by showing a film like *Blade Runner*, which is a dark futuristic vision of a Los Angeles riven by racial, ethnic, extraterrestrial, and class divisions. Follow this by showing *Tank Girl*. The title character of this film, also set during the future and based on a comic book by the same name, is a savvy counterculture guerrilla fighter in a California run by a corporation that hoards natural resources. This film raises questions about power, mixed identity, and sexuality in a funky, funny setting. *Alien II* is another science-fiction thriller about a strong woman who battles both the evil corporate empire and a strange new threat from deep space. Along with these films, you might also consider assigning a novel or two. Octavia E. Butler's 20-minutes-into-the-future take on a dystopian Los Angeles, *Parable of the Sower*, also contains seeds of utopian renewal via community, cooperation, and spirituality. Charlotte Perkins Gilman's 1890s feminist utopia, *Herland*, is interesting to pair with Butler's text because while it contests dominant gender and class roles, it is terrible on race and ethnicity and silent on sexuality. As you go through this section, ask students to consider why the science-fiction genre is chosen so often to portray future change. Also, what do these texts do with gender? Race and ethnicity? Class? Sexuality?

- Part IX also works well when it is paired with depictions of activism. Try showing the documentary *Berkeley in the Sixties* and discuss student activism from free speech to the antiwar movement. You can go even further back and show a film like *Grapes of Wrath* and discuss how it entered into discussions of what to do for poor people during the Great Depression. You can then link this film up to works in other media forms, such as the songs of Woody Guthrie, Bob Dylan, Joan Baez, Pete Seeger, and the like, on to contemporary artist-activists like Ani DiFranco and Bruce Springsteen (whose album *The Ghost of Tom Joad* references both *Grapes of Wrath* and Guthrie's songs, while his recent work, *We Shall Overcome: The Seeger Sessions*, draws on the extensive work of Pete Seeger). *Eyes on the Prize*, or any of the filmed speeches of Dr. Martin Luther King, Jr., speaks to efforts to end racism. All of these texts offer students concrete representations of how people have organized to contest the oppressive structures in which they live.

- For a contemporary, and quite funny, representation of guerrilla activism, rent a tape of some episodes of Michael Moore's *The Awful Truth*. Consult Moore's website for how to get his work. Students will respond to Moore's lively engagement with corporate and public figures, and his unwillingness to allow the status quo to go unchallenged. Ask students whether or not they think this kind of activism is effective and why.

- Another funny and clever way to show individual activism can be found in the documentary, *Supersize Me!* Morgan Spurlock puts himself on a 30-day McDonald's-only diet and then documents what such food does to his body, the environment, children, and the like.

- Show *Norma Rae* and discuss Norma's transformation from an oppressed factory worker to an empowered union organizer in the film. How do Norma and her coworkers benefit materially from her efforts? How is Norma oppressed by her class and gender before her transformation? How does the film deal with race?

- Similarly, show *Salt of the Earth* and discuss how the characters in the film are transformed through their labor activism.

- Ken Loach's film, *Bread and Roses*, is a wonderful fictional depiction of the janitors' struggle to unionize in downtown Los Angeles. In light of recent protests over immigration reform, this film is a corrective to the depictions of Latinos as criminals or "illegals."